ROUTLEDGE LIBRARY EDITIONS:
TRANSPORT ECONOMICS

Volume 12

THE FUNDAMENTALS OF
MANAGEMENT

THE FUNDAMENTALS OF MANAGEMENT
Business Management in Transport 1

W.S. BARRY

Routledge
Taylor & Francis Group

LONDON AND NEW YORK

First published in 1963 by George Allen & Unwin, Ltd.

This edition first published in 2017
by Routledge
2 Park Square, Milton Park, Abingdon, Oxon OX14 4RN

and by Routledge
711 Third Avenue, New York, NY 10017

Routledge is an imprint of the Taylor & Francis Group, an informa business

© 1963 George Allen & Unwin, Ltd.

British Library Cataloguing in Publication Data
A catalogue record for this book is available from the British Library

ISBN: 978-0-415-78484-9 (Set)
ISBN: 978-1-315-20175-7 (Set) (ebk)
ISBN: 978-0-415-79254-7 (Volume 12) (hbk)
ISBN: 978-0-415-79313-1 (Volume 12) (pbk)
ISBN: 978-1-315-21127-5 (Volume 12) (ebk)

Publisher's Note
The publisher has gone to great lengths to ensure the quality of this reprint but points out that some imperfections in the original copies may be apparent.

Disclaimer
The publisher has made every effort to trace copyright holders and would welcome correspondence from those they have been unable to trace.

THE FUNDAMENTALS
OF MANAGEMENT

by W. S. Barry

London

GEORGE ALLEN & UNWIN LTD

RUSKIN HOUSE MUSEUM STREET

FIRST PUBLISHED IN 1963

PRINTED IN GREAT BRITAIN
in 11 on 12 point Times Roman type
BY UNWIN BROTHERS LIMITED
WOKING AND LONDON

PREFACE

Is a textbook on management any use to someone wanting to learn how to manage? Is management a subject that can be written about in such a way that the ideas expressed can be used by a manager? We must treat these questions seriously because there are many experienced managers who say that reading books on management will get the aspiring manager nowhere. These experienced and apparently successful managers argue that management can be learnt only from doing the job, or watching other people doing the job. So they dismiss the idea that a textbook can be of any practicable use.

Not many years ago, experienced and apparently successful surgeons were arguing that surgeons could not be trained by reading books; and they were right. But only if they meant that a surgeon could not be *completely* trained from books. There was a struggle before the surgeon-apprentice, learning solely by standing alongside the master-surgeon, was displaced by the modern college student, who spends hundreds of hours in his books before going to work with a master.

It is the same with management. A manager cannot be trained *completely* by any one or number of books. But it is now widely accepted that the use of a textbook before or alongside his training on the job will help him. Learning solely by experience has proved wasteful in many skilled occupations. Personal experience will in the end always be limited compared with the accumulated experience of great numbers of people set down in writing.

A general textbook for a practical task should indicate the extent of the study that is necessary to accomplish that task. It should draw some boundaries to encompass what is necessary and exclude what is not of immediate concern. It should detail the items of knowledge contained within those boundaries, at least by pointing out the problems, even if it leaves their solution to more specialised works.

The book should also offer a framework in which to fit what might otherwise remain a shapeless body of knowledge. This framework should assist the student by creating a pattern that makes it easier to remember much detail and to relate all the various portions of knowledge. The whole body of knowledge must first be divided logically and with an eye to its eventual use. Then the divisions must be put into an order that leads the reader naturally on from one section to another. My first advice to a student of management would be to take a number of textbooks, examine and note the scheme of study indicated by their Table of Contents. He should ask himself very early on in his studies which framework is likely to serve him best, which gives the clearest picture of the whole field of study and presents it in an orderly fashion so that the whole subject hangs together in his mind once the book is laid aside? I make no claims for the scheme of study suggested by this book beyond the fact that I believe it to be a fresh approach, and that it is the best I could devise in the light of my experience in teaching managers. I do ask that my reader should be critical in his approach to the scheme, and should give careful thought to it before accepting it. The scheme has been explained a little later on because of the great importance I attach to the need for writers on management to solve the problems of mapping out the territory of management studies.

A book can also help by applying to management studies the disciplined processes of analysis and classification. Considerable light may be thrown on the complexities of business, both large and small, by breaking down the complex into its simpler parts. Whole management jobs are made more easily understandable when the separate skills built into them are identified. The human beehive of business organisation looks more purposeful when the important relationships are isolated. In attempting to classify we are compelled to look for common features, which may give rise to similar problems and call for similar treatment. So we may group together certain tasks, certain individuals' authority, certain human attributes in an endeavour to *marshal* our ideas before having to make an on-the-spot decision; and, of course, books must lead to this—decision! Analysis and classification must not be carried to the lengths of robbing a manager of his ability to make a decision.

Finally a management textbook should help to establish the language of management studies. It is inevitable that managers, like those engaged in every other branch of human activity, should consider their mother tongue as a living language. They will employ words in everyday use in a special sense for their own particular purposes. Only rarely will they create entirely new words. For this reason there is a clear need for writers to proceed warily in their employment of words, so that they are understood in their special sense, and not in their ordinary everyday sense.

These considerations have led me to restate much that is not original. But if the restatement is more clear and more concise than what has gone before it will not be wasted. Some of the ideas expressed in this work are new to the literature of management. Certainly some of the analyses and classifications are original and may not in the end prove generally acceptable. But an effort has been made to see that all unfamiliar terms are well defined.

Ordinarily a body of knowledge is called a 'subject' if it is recognised as a *separate department* of knowledge. It took a long time for universities to recognise geography as a subject because scholars argued that it did no more than gather together material from other departments of learning. They were referring to subjects like geology, oceanography, meteorology and so on. There was nothing in geography that was not a subject in its own right. There was no purely geographical knowledge.

Some people argued that geography should be considered a subject because of the *particular use* it made of the knowledge it borrowed from a number of sciences. Geography took knowledge from other departments and welded it into a new pattern. This rearrangement was useful because it brought together all those items of knowledge necessary to explain why the places in which men live are what they are. It helped men to create what may be called a philosophy of place. In a sense geography is an applied science, drawing on the pure sciences of geology, geomorphology and others.

But what science is a pure science, except pure mathematics? Geology borrows from physics and chemistry. These in their turn borrow from mathematics. So the exclusion of geography on these grounds is discriminating. Deciding whether a field of study is a subject by what it borrows from other subjects is unsatisfactory.

It has been argued that there is no reason to put such diverse subjects as accountancy, economics, statistics, law and psychology into one subject called management. We may follow the geographer's lead and point out that management as a subject makes something new by bringing together parts of

A*

these recognised branches of learning. This rearrangement is also useful because it brings together items of knowledge necessary to explain why men 'manage' as they do. Management is a department of knowledge in which other subjects are related to the affairs of men in business.

But what is there about the affairs of men in business that still needs to be explained? Have not the economists done most of the explaining? And has not the rest been done by the accountants, statisticians and psychologists?

None of them have really dealt with management because management is, among other things, the art of bringing all their contributions into a workable whole. Combining their skills is part of *the skill of organising*. Organising business is an act of management that makes a fitting subject for study.

Other forms of organisation have been studied for a long while. Some of the earliest writings of men dealt with the organisation of state and the study has been pursued in greater depth down to the present day. Politics is a respectable and accepted form of study. Military organisation is studied with equal care. No modern army could face the future with confidence, misplaced or otherwise, if its senior officers had not made a study of the adequacy and inadequacy of military organisations of the past in the light of their circumstances.

Economists set out to provide a rational and disciplined approach to the study of business. The debt that any writer on management owes to economists is very great, and it is one that is too seldom acknowledged. That economists did not go further is due partly to the attempts of early economists to limit their field of study. Because of the criticisms of scholars in already accepted disciplines, economists were anxious to get the new social science established, by creating palpably clear boundaries. This endeavour drove some of them to restrictions from which the study is still suffering. The particular abstraction of *homo economicus* was probably the most constricting. It certainly left the door open for an ill-disciplined treatment of a topic that became known as 'human relations', with a main premise that money was not the sole motive for man's actions. In general, economists had never said it was, but writers assumed otherwise. Economists did not say that man was all money-motive, but set out to explain the workings of the money-motive in every man.

Organisation is then a thread that must run through the whole subject of management. We still have to decide how best to divide the subject up to allow an orderly and logical approach to it. Organisation is essentially a task of getting relationships right. These relationships in business fall into three distinct groups that provide natural divisions of study. Firstly there are the relationships between those inside the business organisation and those outside it. Secondly, there are the relationships between various parts of the business, between man and man, and among men, equipment and raw materials. And thirdly, there are the relationships of the different parts of the individual manager, his different qualities or characteristics, and desires that may interfere with one another.

We may draw a useful analogy from the relationships of an orchestra. Firstly there is the relationship between the orchestra and the audience. Someone has to decide what piece of music the whole orchestra will play to please the listeners. Secondly, each player must come in at the right moment in order to combine the notes into the complete piece of music, and thirdly, each performer's individual instrument must be in tune.

The scheme of this work emphasises the importance of organisation in the work of management, and follows the lines of relationships described above. It examines first the group of management's external relations with the customer, state, shareholders, suppliers, and public. The second part deals with the internal relations of management, where organisation requires a great amount of attention. This part is divided into three sections, treating internal relations separately from the standpoints of organisation, industrial relations, general and special management. The third part deals with the individual manager.

I must end by emphasising that there are other ways of dividing the subject up, but that I hope this way will help men and women who are striving to improve their understanding of management in the interest of their fellows.

June 30, 1962   W. S. B.

ACKNOWLEDGEMENTS

Even if I have failed to turn their help to good account I should like to thank those who gave it. To three men, Sir William Robson-Brown, Mr Anthony Milward and Mr Cyril Herring, I owe the opportunities I have had to work among managers in business. I am indebted to my colleagues in British European Airways for many enlightening hours of discussion. Mr George White and Mr Ted Gregory helped me by reading and criticising my manuscript, and my wife patiently endured the trials of preparing each fresh draft.

CONTENTS

PART III   THE INDIVIDUAL MANAGER

SUMMARY

Part I
External Relations of Management

CHAPTER I
RELATIONS WITH CUSTOMERS

CHAPTER II
RELATIONS WITH THE STATE

CHAPTER III

RELATIONS WITH SHAREHOLDERS, SUPPLIERS AND PUBLIC

The Shareholder

Meeting the shareholder.
Factors affecting the power of shareholders.
The right of the individual shareholder.
Balancing the interests of shareholders and the business organisation.

Suppliers
The Public

Who are the public?
The way distribution distinguishes the roles of customer and public.
The public relations officer.

CHAPTER IV

ORGANISATION AND EXTERNAL RELATIONS

Specialists in the external relations of a business.
The positions of Chairman and Managing Director.
The ways that business organisation can annoy the outsider.
The impression that morale makes on outsiders.

Part II

Internal Relations of Management

SECTION I—ORGANISATION

CHAPTER V

ELEMENTS OF ORGANISATION

Is organisation separable from business?
Everyday meaning of organisation.
Organisations are instruments.
The comparison with a piano.
Men, equipment, raw materials.
Objects of change, agents of change, operatives.
The connections between elements of organisation.
Processes of setting up a business organisation.
Common causes of failure of business organisation.

Seven main physical factors that are thought to influence productivity, contentment and health.
What the worker regards as essential to the main purpose of his work.
Trade Union representatives and labour relations officers.
Differences among trade unions.

SECTION III—GENERAL AND SPECIAL MANAGEMENT

CHAPTER XII

THE NATURE AND TASK OF GENERAL MANAGEMENT

The distinction between general and special management.
Three positions of general management—
Chairman, Board of Directors, Managing Director.
General Manager's relations with superior special managers.
General Manager's relations with subordinate special managers.
Three main causes of failure in relationship between general managers and special managers.
Further weaknesses in general management.
Recruitment of general managers.
Difficulties at the connection between general and special managers.

CHAPTER XIII

FINANCE MANAGEMENT

Summary of the main financial activities.
Furnishing the capital of business.
Protecting the capital of business.
Making it easy for lenders to withdraw their capital.
Determining the price to be paid for lenders' money.
Feeding money into the organisation.
Seeing that money fed into the organisation is not wasted or used in an unauthorised manner.
Calculating and distributing profit.
Establishing sound book-values.
Choosing and using good accounting tools.
Controlling accounting, statistical and bookkeeping staff.

CHAPTER XIV

PURCHASING MANAGEMENT

Relationship between purchasing manager and production manager.
The purchase of capital equipment.
Purchasing and stocking spares.
Purchasing manager's relationships governed by contract.
Buying raw materials. Four basic approaches.
Grouping of buyers.

Part III

The Individual Manager

Examination results as evidence of development.
School reports.
Choosing people from another or one's own business.
Value of business records as evidence of development.
Early years in business often a bad environment.
The value of continuing academic studies during 'routine' years.
Development of disposition in business.
Development of skill and knowledge.
Experience the teacher—but it must be illuminated by theory.
A development programme.

CHAPTER XXI

REWARDS FOR MANAGERS

The need to give some thought to the subject.
The argument for leaving the matter to natural economic forces.
The fallacy in believing that the supply of managers is narrowly restricted.
Discouraging the self-seeker.
Need to avoid wasting managerial abilities.

Part I

External Relations of Management

'We may fling ourselves into a hammock in
a fit of divine carelessness; but we are glad
that the maker did not make the hammock
in a fit of divine carelessness.'

G. K. CHESTERTON

INTRODUCTION

This section has been placed before sections on internal relations and the individual manager for a reason. It is a case of putting first things first. Every business owes its beginning to those who put things into it, and it owes its survival to those who take things out of it. The reason for the existence of a business lies in the opinion of the community in whose midst it is. The external relations talked about in the next four chapters are not just one part of business relations that can be treated like any other part. The external relations of business are not like the foreign relations of a state: the latter are often nuisances to be endured and can be minimised by pursuing a policy of isolation.

The external relations of business are the fount of all relationships. Although we discuss internal relations separately it must not be thought that they have an independent existence. To avoid error it is necessary to recall constantly that the three sets of relationships that form the basis of division of this work are very interdependent.

CHAPTER I

RELATIONS WITH CUSTOMERS

It is worth while for any manager of a business, or part of a business, to give some thought to the extent and nature of his dealings with his customers. How often should he meet them, speak to them on the telephone, or exchange letters with them? Should he seek out his customers or wait for them to come to him? Should he regard his relations with them as continuous or for the time being? If he does deal personally with customers a manager will probably want to set some limits to his dealings by deciding that beyond a certain point he will hand over to subordinates.

Let us take four examples. Mr Smith is a bank manager. Customers ask to see him whenever they feel they need his help or advice. Many of his most valuable customers are farmers and he often spends an afternoon looking around their farms. Smith regards it as part of his job to pay occasional visits to the local pub and join local groups like the Rotary Club. He sees very little of the clerks in the bank and leaves the internal organisation of the branch almost entirely to his chief clerk.

Jones is the captain of an ocean-going passenger ship. He meets some of the passengers each evening at dinner. He also lets it be known that he is available at short notice to see any passenger on matters of importance. A request to see the captain must be put through the Purser's Office, and the purser may exercise his own discretion as to whether he passes it on or not. Jones does not expect interviews with passengers to interfere much with what he regards as the primary job of keeping the ship afloat and heading in the right direction.

Brown is a shift manager in a steel-smelting shop. Very occasionally a senior person from one of the customer-firms comes round to take a look at his shop. He wonders what they learn from such a visit, but if his own company thinks it is of value then he is content to put up with the inconvenience. He says that the customer gets exactly what he asks for and there is the end of the matter. There are enough analysts around the place to make doubly sure that the steel is up to specification.

Williams is the manager of a retail store. He has an office at the back of the shop and expects to talk to customers only when they insist upon seeing the manager, usually for purposes of making complaints. Sometimes Williams strolls around the store to see for himself how customers are treated by the sales women.

There are no golden rules to guide any of these men. Each has to make up his mind how much personal attention he will give to customer relations compared with attention given to internal and other external relations. The nature of his business may well determine how much freedom of choice he has in the matter, but very rarely is the need for good judgement entirely removed.

At one end of the scale we have business that sells services like transport, entertainment and dentistry. These differ from businesses that sell goods like saucepans and armchairs in that the former usually require a customer to take delivery at the moment of production. So that for example no matter how absorbed he is in his techniques the hairdresser must meet his customers.

Where the service that is sold is a rare skill possessed only, or in exceptional measure, by the manager of a business, he has little choice but to devote most of his time to the customer. He is in a similar position if he does not possess exceptional skill, but is reputed to do so. A lawyer with a high reputation would find it hard to convince a client that he should consult one of his more able subordinates and leave him to get on with running the office. This situation is common to all forms of professional business, e.g. architects, schools, medical clinics and industrial consultants. In most businesses of this sort we find that responsibility for their inner workings is placed upon someone referred to as an administrative assistant or chief clerk.

Managers in some businesses producing goods find themselves in the same position, fundamentally for the same reason. Although aircraft manufacturers and fashion houses produce tangible goods their chief designers are in much the same position in relation to the customer as the lawyer or dentist. Although he may be the head of a large design department he leaves the internal running to someone else to conserve his time and energy for the rarer creative skills.

But at the other end of the scale are those businesses selling goods that require considerable skill in their production. Among them, for example, are the small craftsmen businesses, like small building firms, watch repairing, where customer relations are left to the girl in the office or at the counter. Also among them are bigger highly technical mass production firms whose processes demand the severe concentration of a single-minded man.

But for most managers the issues are not so clear cut. They are left to wonder whether they have achieved the right balance in their relations with customers. A common cause of failure among them is a preoccupation with technical processes that blinds them to changes that are taking place in the needs of customers, or they allow customers to waste their time and prevent them from giving much needed attention to the discipline of their staff and good order of their equipment.

Any relationship between a manager and his customers is reflected elsewhere in the business. Some of the possible repercussions are:

1. Customers who are acquainted with the manager acquire importance in the eyes of his subordinates. If a manager singles out a few customers for his special attention this is likely to result in their receiving exceptional treatment from his staff. Other customers who observe this may be very irritated by it.

2. Some customers will take full advantage of an acquaintanceship with the manager and abuse the relationship by using it to intimidate in their dealings with subordinates. They may even indulge in unfair practices backed by the feeling that they will be protected by higher authority if they run into trouble.

3. A manager may be tempted to adopt a policy of siding with the customer in all cases of complaint. This attitude may be associated with the widespread myth 'that the customer is always right'. While this fiction has been extremely useful in establishing some fine traditions of service it should not be used against staff. They have the right to justice in the investigation of any complaint and the settlement of any dispute.

4. A policy of always insisting that staff are in the right is no better. At times it will produce obvious injustices to the customer. It is irritating for the customer and, in the end, corrupting for staff.

5. A manager who uses customers' reports or complaints as a source of information about the efficiency of his staff runs certain dangers. A person who is buying something, whether it be goods or services, is in a special situation in which feelings are apt to run high. Almost every purchaser has at the back of his mind the idea of a bargain in which he has come out on top, or not, and human emotions of every sort flit across the market-place. So customers' views of the nature of a transaction should always be suspect as lacking in objectivity.

A manager is very likely to run into trouble with his staff if he listens to reports from customers and does not at once let his staff know what has been said. Subordinates find it intensely disturbing to live with the knowledge that their manager is a repository for complaints that go unanswered. Secret charges are considered reprehensible in most civilised communities and laws usually provide for specific charges to be made openly and answered openly.

A manager who works for part of his time as a salesman may avoid some of these dangers, especially if it is not apparent to the customer that he is the manager. A merchandise manager in a big and famous London store believes that it is necessary for him to spend at least half his working time serving customers as an ordinary salesman. By this means he has first-hand information on what his customers think of his wares; he experiences the difficulties of a salesman and remains sympathetic with them, and in working alongside his subordinates he learns much about them.

One of the penalties of becoming a manager may be that a man is deprived of the pleasure that accompanies the employment of a personal skill. For this reason it is tempting to find some justification for slipping back into the role of an operative. This must be watched by the manager who is spending part of his time 'doing the job'. He may be quite right in a belief that by doing so he is improving his managing, but if he is wrong he is an unnecessarily expensive salesman.

The idea that a word with the customer is useful as a check on the satisfactoriness of his unit is not confined to managers on the sales side of business. In many airlines captains of aircraft make a practice of checking passengers' reactions to their cabin and operating procedures. This sort of check is one that could be useful to specialist managers. Why should not a Chief Accountant talk with his 'customers', within the organisation he serves, to ensure that his accounting procedures are not unnecessarily cumbersome?

The need for this sort of check is not so great if the manager is also a consumer of his own product. A man who uses one of the motor-cars he makes for other people may possibly get a valuable insight into the opinions of his customers unless, of course, his own tastes are not representative of the taste of his customers. A wine-merchant retailing his wines in an industrial, predominantly beer-drinking area, might be led very much astray by forming opinions of his customers' reactions from his own sampling.

One of the points a manager must always remember is that his attitude towards customers will usually be taken as an example of the way a customer should be treated. The example may not always be followed, but it will tend to stand as a norm. If the example is a bad one it will be used openly or secretly as a justification for a subordinate behaving badly at some time or another.

In his dealings with a customer a manager is not on the same legal footing as are his subordinates. In the eyes of the law a manager is distinguished from his subordinates by the greater scope of his authority. This scope of authority is of great significance when it comes to considering the powers an employee has to bind his employer.

Does any manager know the extent to which he is able to commit his employer? Is it for £10,000 or merely £10? He may gain some idea from his terms of reference if he has any, or he may know that he is expressly authorised by a higher authority to incur expenditure up to a certain limit. His power to bind the firm is not strictly bound by his express authority so far as the customer is concerned, unless the customer is aware of the restrictions on it. In the absence of express restrictions, of which the customer has notice, servants have power to bind their masters within the scope of their ostensible authority. This means that, at a meeting of customer and manager, the latter's express authority may have less legal consequences than the authority that is implied by his appearance, bearing, title and past conduct in that capacity.

If a customer goes to see a man called a managing director, whose dress, room and furnishings indicate that he is a man of high rank in the company, the customer is entitled to assume that the man he sees has very wide powers.

So if a manager in an ill-considered exchange goes beyond his express authority, his company may still be bound to honour his undertakings. In other words, the internal regulations of the company do not entirely govern the legal relationship between manager and customer. A breach of internal regulations may gain the company no more than the right to take disciplinary action against the manager-errant. The manager, by exceeding his authority, does, of course, incur personal liability, for breach of warranty of authority, for any loss the customer may suffer.

The personal relations between managers in monopolistic undertakings and their customers have special difficulties. A hasty word, or slightest show of indifference from the manager, all too often is interpreted as a sign of arrogance, bred in the belief that it does not matter. A customer is suspicious and constantly on the lookout for evidence of the manager taking advantage of his relatively strong position. The customer is conscious of the weakness of his position, where, if he does not like it, he can lump it.

Some big organisations appoint a special manager to deal with Customer Relations. He is found under various titles, among them Consumer Relations Manager, Passenger Relations Manager, Public Relations Manager and even Complaints Manager. The last but one title is misleading because it usually refers to something else; to the public at large, rather than the small section who are customers. In this way monopolies are able to minimise the dangers referred to above. A manager who lives day by day with the explosive nature of ill-chosen words is likely to be more successful in avoiding danger.

The terms of reference of such specialists vary a little. Some of them are responsible for answering all customer complaints. This usually involves looking into the circumstances that gave rise to the complaint and letting those concerned know that a complaint has been made, so that they can make any improvements that are possible. Answers to customers range from those that unashamedly set out to mollify by hiding the truth, to those that give full explanations of the cause of the trouble, with information on how it is proposed to prevent recurrence. From a business point of view the second approach can land the customer-relations specialist in as much trouble as the first, by sparking off an endless correspondence on technicalities only imperfectly understood by the customer.

Some customer-relations managers are required to deal only with those complaints that involve a number of departments in their organisation. This saves the customer going from one department to another in order to obtain full satisfaction. Also the various contributions are brought together to avoid the dangers of piecemeal explanations to the customer. It is often considered equally important for a specialist to deal with all complaints that involve policy of the whole business, but as policy is very seldom expressed as such it makes a vague definition of duties.

Finally, there is the idea that all complaints should be dealt with uniformly. This precaution is very necessary if it is the practice to fob customers off with the first excuse that springs to mind.

Another stage in the formalising of the relationship between managers and customers is the creation of a Consumers' Council on which sit representatives of producers and consumers. Many managers find that these are not satisfactory substitutes for the personal relations they expect to have anyway. They also find sometimes that the people who sit on consumers' councils are not really representative of their customers and are much more likely to be representing sectional interests. On the other hand customers do sometimes need protecting. Some managements are unscrupulous, and take advantage of the ignorance of their customers concerning the technicalities of their product. And why should not customers get together for mutual protection when business men constantly seek to strengthen their position by alliances of one sort or another?

B

CHAPTER II

RELATIONS WITH
THE STATE

The relations between managers and their customers depend very much on the attitudes of managers. The power to make changes that improve or impair relations is mainly in the hands of managers. With managers and the State it is different. The machinery of State is too big and too powerful for the individual manager to alter. Members of parliament, judges and government officials are more easily influenced by public opinion than by the opinions of a small section of the community. So the relations between managers and the State are more often usefully described in terms of broad governmental policies and less often in terms of individual attitudes. This is particularly true when talking about the more usual dealings with government officials who, in England, move frequently from post to post, and with ease from ministry to ministry.

In England in the nineteenth century, the *laissez-faire* policy of government restricted the activities of officials and guarded the boundaries of an area of very considerable freedom in the employers' internal and external relations. In theory the State assumed the role of a policeman standing on the edge of an arena to ensure that no one interfered with the contest inside it. The competitors were farmers, manufacturers, workpeople and customers, and the rules of the competition were those enshrined in the idea of Free Trade. The policeman was also there to prevent competitors from provoking breaches of the peace and from committing crimes. He was there to ensure the law and order necessary for an unobstructed working of the natural economic processes. The manager's relations with others were supposed to be well regulated by what was called enlightened self-interest. The self was the manager's self, and the reference to 'enlightened' betrayed a naïve belief in the self-restraint of managers. The idea was bound up with the economic theory that in working for his own benefit an individual inevitably created wealth for others.

There was some substance in the idea. The community as a whole was enriched by the steady accumulation of capital. But building up resources for producing can only be achieved by forgoing immediate enjoyment. Many managers in those times had a sense of stewardship, and were abstemious in their personal habits, but even so the contrast between their sacrifices and those of the workpeople was too great. The employment of women and young children in coalmines, a working day of fourteen to sixteen hours for men and the provision of unhealthy workshops was overstepping the mark. There was an element of dash and daring in the idea of free trade, but a free-for-all in production led to sordid exploitation. The State had to step into the ring.

The intervention of the State did not at once embitter relations between State and managers. Acts of Parliament that limited hours of work, prohibited dangerous and unhealthy working conditions, and prescribed minimum wages did no more than control the worst abuses of the worst employers. They were not greatly resented by the majority of fair-minded employers, many of whom were relieved to be rid of the need to compete amid a welter of human misery. But in order to get in the right perspective the early development in England of relations between employers and the State, we must consider the effects of the anti-Jacobin measures of the first quarter of the nineteenth century. During this period any banding together of workpeople for any purpose was punishable as sedition. Trevelyan[1] says 'to leave the workman unprotected by the State as to wages, hours and factory conditions, while denying him the right to protect himself by combination was frankly unjust. It was not *laissez-faire*, but liberty for the masters and repression for the men.'

Although the anti-Jacobin spirit seemed to have subsided by 1824 when the Combination Laws were repealed, the close alliance of State and employer was renewed by the attitude of the government as shown in the prosecution of the Tolpuddle Martyrs in 1834.

[1] *English Social History.*

Common Law protection for employers had been restored a year after the 1824 Act, and it was not until 1871 that managers lost the protection of the Common Law prohibition against acts in restraint of trade.

The 1875 Conspiracy and Protection of Property Act further revealed the extent of legal comfort that the employer had enjoyed. It permitted joint action in contemplation of furtherance of a trade dispute unless such an action by an individual would have been punishable as a crime. In other words, an otherwise lawful act did not become criminal just because people banded together to perform it! The 1901 Taff Vale Judgement of the House of Lords was a swing back to the side of the employers. It exposed Unions to actions for damages in Civil Courts for wrongs done by its agents during a strike, and the damages would have to be paid out of union funds.

The Trade Disputes Act of 1906 was the State's final recognition that employees needed more help in their industrial relations than did the managers. It permitted work people to do things that would otherwise be illegal, and exempted them from having to pay damages they would otherwise have to pay.

This is history. But it is against this background that managers have to consider their relations with the State today. Many may ask if the State has not gone too far in stripping them of legal protection. Are not employees in association too powerful because of their privileged position in law? Are not the employers too weak? Is it just that an employer is not able to take action against people who induce others to break a contract of employment? This and a number of other questions worry managers who sincerely wish for justice to all parties. But their reading of history must convince them that there are equal dangers in the State allying itself too closely with employers. Putting the clock back can only be a matter of small movement.

We must also remember that towards the end of the nineteenth century employers themselves began to attack the very idea of free trade. They began to look for the sort of State protection for markets that was produced by the mercantilist policy of the Elizabethan era. But the Elizabethan government had not only protected employers but built elaborate statutory control over their treatment of workpeople. Neo-mercantilists did not succeed in getting the one without the other. If the State is invited in to help in one way it becomes more difficult to resist its unwelcome intrusion in other ways.

That these lessons of history have been well learnt is amply illustrated by the attitude of managers today. For example, there is the managing director of a large organisation who will not accept a State subsidy to cover an unprofitable but socially important service his company provides, because he does not wish to open the doors to the government controls that accompany a subsidy. Many managers believe that any attempt to enlist the support of the State to further their own particular ends, however worthy they may be, is likely to cause more mischief than it remedies. Many trade-union leaders agree that manipulation of government is a less satisfactory approach to their problems than is industrial action. By the latter they mean negotiation, threats and strikes. But there were many managers who, during the 1961 wage 'pause' imposed by Selwyn Lloyd, the Chancellor of the Exchequer, spoke about the undesirability of the government's interference in free negotiation. There has developed since 1945 a considerable body of opinion even in government circles that the only relations the State should have with either side is that of impartial mediator. Is this a truer version of the spirit of *laissez-faire*?

Not that all managers have given up the idea that it is useful to enlist the sympathies of government officials and members of parliament. The late 'fifties' in England saw the rapid growth of public relations agencies who specialised in 'fixing' members of parliament and government officials. They claimed that a knowledgeable and skilful intermediary could greatly help the manager in his relations with the State. It was argued that many troubles arose simply because the manager did not know his way around the complicated machinery of State, did not go to the right people at the right time, and so on. One or two members of parliament were to be found at the head of agencies.

What is a sensible view for a manager to take to what he may well regard as State interference in his business? The extent and nature of the statutory regulations and orders in council vary, of course, from business to business. But all businesses are subject to some.

First of all it is necessary to face the fact that there were usually very good reasons for making the regulations, and in most cases there are equally good reasons for their continuing.

History shows that employers were capable of abusing the power they had over people at work, and a minority of managers continue to illustrate that it is dangerous to leave too much power in their hands. The State plays an important part in industry in checking these abuses. I have dwelt on governments' concern to prevent the exploitation of workpeople, but I am mindful of the achievements of government in preventing some employers from callously disregarding the damage they do to the amenities of a community. We are all aware of the need for the State regulations designed to protect consumers from misrepresentation and carelessness.

Secondly, we should recognise that the State, in pursuing its policy of protecting workpeople, consumers and communities, is also guarding good employers from unfair competition. More often than not exploitation means reducing costs of production by shifting on to somebody, who should not be called upon to bear it, a burden that should be borne by the business. Lower production costs are very telling in any struggle between business competitors.

If we agree that State intervention is on balance a good thing, then we should face the logical necessity of the State employing inspectors to enforce its regulations. Government inspectors and business managers have in general learnt to get on with each other remarkably well. This is in no small degree due to the enlightened outlook of inspectors in recent years. At one time a government inspector was often a badly paid employee whose promotion was dependent upon the number of successful prosecutions. He was rightly regarded as a snooper, rapporteur and prosecutor. Now inspectors are very often welcomed into factories as advisers. They are taught to regard the main importance of their work as being that of encouraging good practices and warning against bad practices. Usually they no longer try to catch an employer out in the unintentional small infringements, but concentrate on the deliberate and dangerous evasions.

In 1960 a number of managers of the General Electric Company were sent to prison by a United States Federal Court for breaking the anti-trust laws. These laws made illegal certain acts that were construed as being acts to limit industrial competition. This sort of act would not be regarded as criminal by the ordinary citizen in most countries of the western world. He would probably agree that governments had to do something to check the growth of industrial empires. But the news of otherwise respectable managers being cast into gaol shocked very many people. It was treating them like common criminals for what was after all no more than a technical offence. Some people argued that if the law wanted to demonstrate individual responsibility it could have achieved it by levying fines instead of imposing prison sentences; then at least the unfortunate victims could have been reimbursed by their company.

Why should not the law punish a manager for the infringement of laws relevant to his office? Why should he escape the consequences of his acts because he is regarded as an agent and not a principal? It is interesting to speculate on the probable effects on managerial behaviour if the State were to take a more severe view of managers' personal responsibility.

The interdependence of State and management is increasing. On the one hand managers rely more and more on the services of government agencies, offering credit, supplying statistics, producing forecasts and conducting research. On the other hand the State relies on managers to provide essential services that are as important to the maintenance of social order as are police forces and armies. At many points in the fabric of a modern community, managements' economic responsibility coincides with the State's political responsibilities.

Nowhere is this more clearly illustrated than in the conduct of nationalised industries, and here new ideas of public accountability are being hammered out in the fierce light of the publicity that is given to all important acts of management. Managers in nationalised industries are more exposed to public criticism than are their colleagues in private industry. Questions in parliament, courts of enquiry and press reports are effective means of bringing home to a manager that he is personally responsible for his mistakes. Most men feel keenly the stigma of a bad press.

Finally, we must come back to the effect of a state's doctrinal approach to the subject of 'freedom of trade'. This always has been, and continues to be, one of the most important grounds for State interference in business management. Some countries do all they can to avoid what they regard as the evils of competitive business. Others are concerned to see that trade is as free as possible. In England the investigations of the Monopolies Commission are in keeping with our traditional dislike of cartels.

CHAPTER III

RELATIONS WITH SHAREHOLDERS
SUPPLIERS AND PUBLIC

The Shareholder

To be fair we must acknowledge the stake a shareholder has in a business. But if the relations between managers and shareholders are to remain healthy the stake must be recognised for what it is. It must be given its rightful place, and no more, among all the other stakes in a business. We have heard of elderly widows whose all is sunk in a business, and whose fate depends upon the decision of managers. On the other hand, there are managers who have devoted the best years of their lives to a business whose fate depends upon the decision of shareholders; for example, during a take-over bid. The interests of shareholders and managers are common to a certain extent, but experience teaches us that there are always areas in which interests conflict.

The entire capital of a small business may be owned by two or three people who appoint a manager for the day-to-day running of the business. For example, it often happens that a working father leaves a business to his sons who look to a manager as a way of getting a more leisurely life than that enjoyed by their father. But sometimes their anxiety to protect the leisured life impels them to keep a close watch on the wretched manager. His life is made exceedingly difficult by constant and untimely visits from one or other of his 'shareholders'.

A manager in a medium-sized company may find himself at the other extreme. He may go his whole career without ever meeting, speaking or writing to anyone he knew to be a shareholder. He may entirely ignore the existence of shareholders or regard them as very important persons to be dealt with by the managing director or the secretary.

A manager in one of the business giants is not normally in either of these situations. It is likely that the shares in his company are spread among tens of thousands of people up and down the country. If the industrial giant is a nationalised industry very many more people may regard themselves as shareholders in some sense. So such a manager may bump into a shareholder when taking his half-pint at the local pub, or he may even find that some of his own subordinates are shareholders.

From the point of view of the manager, the important difference in the manager-shareholder relationship from one business to another is the power of the two parties. A manager is not so concerned whether he meets shareholders socially, or occasionally at business, or never at all, but he is very concerned with the amount of control they exercise. The amount of control they exercise must, to his mind, be at the expense of his freedom to do what he thinks is right.

Not all shareholders want to breathe down the necks of managers. Some of them take the very reasonable view that a manager's job is not one in which a man can be goaded. But apart from the personal preferences of shareholders, the relationship is governed by a number of other factors. The ability of a shareholder to make his weight felt must depend upon the proportion he holds of the total shares held in the company. Less significant, unless shares are fairly evenly distributed, is the total number of shareholders. The motive to interfere tends to be strongest where the shares held by a shareholder represent the greater portion of his income. A man who knows that his own livelihood is tied to the fate of a business will normally take a lively interest in it. The collective power of shareholders is affected by the degree of unity among them. This unity is rarely a deep and lasting phenomenon. It is usually manufactured for short periods and is based upon specific issues. In the same way, very sharp divisions may be created.

There are two circumstances that overawe shareholders and make them feel that they had better trust the management or get out. The first is where the assets of a business are made to grow rather mysteriously out of reserves. Perhaps the individual shareholder feels that if a business has provided some of its own capital from its earnings it owes him less. After all, is he not benefiting from this 'growth'? Perhaps he has never

B*

questioned the rights and wrongs of withholding profits from him to put into reserve. The second is where work in the business is very highly skilled and the process of production difficult to understand. The government is in the same position with the nationalised industries. It is less able to interfere with the day-to-day running of those that are technically complex.

A manager's beliefs about the rights of individual shareholders must affect his conduct in business. Because the interests of individual shareholders sometimes conflict with the well-being of other people concerned with a business, managers have to make decisions in favour of one or the other. I am using the term 'individual shareholders' to avoid thinking about shareholders in general. The latter are fictional characters who never take their money out of a business, who never die and are thus willing to take very long-term views. I am talking about those people who have ideas of keeping their money in a business for ten or twenty years, and who want to see some benefit in their own lifetime. A manager's beliefs about their rights are very important to these people.

Firstly, it is reasonable for a shareholder to expect that a manager will exercise all his skill to protect the one thing he has put into the business—his money. The law does its best to protect that money from the dishonest, but does little or nothing to protect it from the foolish or the irresponsible. Putting money into a business involves risk. A shareholder cannot expect to escape the possibility of loss in what is, after all, a commercial gamble. But he should be able to rely upon managers taking a responsible attitude to risk-taking.

It is tempting to argue from this that the shareholders should always be kept well informed on the state of a business so that they may use their own judgement to salvage what they can when things begin to look bad. But managers cannot take such a one-sided view. They are responsible for other people besides shareholders. How is a manager to know that shareholders will not panic at the first sign of trouble, and wreck a business by rushing to withdraw their money? This might well mean that many men lose their jobs unnecessarily because the setback would only have been temporary. Managers may reasonably take the view that a shareholder in putting money into a business sets going a chain of events from which he cannot extricate himself at a moment's notice. The law may have limited his liability to the extent of his shareholding, but it is not the job of management to complete this protection.

One would equally wish that there were some code to prevent managers from withdrawing their personal stakes in business at very short notice. A manager who leaves suddenly, taking with him know-how, probably acquired at the expense of share-holders, can do a lot of damage to a business, and shareholders have not the same means of keeping his skill in the business as he has of keeping their money in the business.

Shareholders often think that managers are too bold in the use of money that is not their own. This idea usually stems from a failure to understand the fundamental distinction between income and capital expenditure. On the other hand, managers often complain that the board representatives of shareholders are too cautious in their approach to new ideas.

Managers are particularly critical of what they regard as attempts to milk a business dry. This they see as a practice that stunts the growth of the business and involves the risk of its sudden failure, through lack of adequate reserves which should have been built up from ploughed-back profits.

There is the opposite view sometimes held by shareholders that managers have devious means of avoiding a complete share-out of the spoils. Feelings have run very high when what was regarded as a deliberate management policy to benefit the business at the expense of individual shareholders is exposed by the circumstances surrounding a take-over bid.

The presenting of accounts, and describing the state of a business at a meeting of shareholders can still be the most effective way of regulating the relations between management and shareholders. The idea of providing the facts in figures to show precisely what has happened to a money stake is sound. That such a review should be confined to regular and not too frequent intervals is prudent. But that the delivery should be in archaic accounting form is preposterous. Some annual accounts are now put in a narrative fashion that can be understood by someone who is not a trained accountant. Some annual reports honestly attempt to reveal the truth rather than resort to the comforting obscurity of convention.

Suppliers

With the money obtained from customers and shareholders, a

business buys its essential supplies. These may range from minor items of stationery through to large machines, or from a few dozen nuts and bolts to a hundred thousand plates of steel. The number of suppliers of equipment and raw materials for even a small business is usually surprisingly large. Probably many of these suppliers are not particularly valuable in that they can easily be replaced. Other suppliers could be found to provide exactly the same things, so that a business has some cause to be indifferent as to which suppliers it has. On the other hand there are a few suppliers who are vital to a business in the sense that they cannot readily be replaced, and unless an alternative to a defecting supplier were found promptly the business would suffer damage through shortage of supplies.

The relationship between the managers of a business and its suppliers is one that calls for careful attention. A manager who buys carelessly and pays more for supplies than he needs to do, places a burden on all parts of his business. If supplies impose extra costs on business, either its customers must bear them or some part of the business organisation must make economies to offset them. If he is to take proper care in buying a manager needs to cultivate an attitude of wariness in his relationship with suppliers. It is not a relationship in which he can relax in the full knowledge that his supplier will never deliberately let him down. This is because the matter does not rest within the deliberation of the individual supplier. He is, himself, part of a competitive situation. A competitor can put him in the shade, and make him comparatively costly to a customer whose interests he may have very much at heart. A business must not allow the fact that it has been buying raw materials cheaply for a number of years from the same supplier to lull it into the belief that it will always be so. If I am buying raw materials at 6d. a unit, blind to the fact that my competitor is quietly buying at 5d. a unit elsewhere, I may soon be run out of business.

Besides keeping a close eye on what his supplier's competitors are doing, a manager must watch the progress of his supplier's own business. He must learn to diagnose its difficulties in order to distinguish the normal from the serious, and when he discovers the serious he must make plans to switch with the minimum of delay to another supplier.

The relationship between a business and its suppliers is often regarded as being so important that it is entrusted to a special manager. The task of the purchasing manager is treated in more detail in Chapter XIV.

The Public

It is interesting to speculate on what is meant by the 'public' or 'general public' from the point of view of industry. There are a number of industrial public relations officers who are uncertain about it, but I am assuming that one man may occupy the roles of customer, shareholder and member of the public at the same or different times. For example, I am a customer as I am enjoying the warmth from an electric fire, but I have other enjoyments, other interests, not derived from the electricity company. Thus I may, as a member of the public, which suggests that I am not behaving as a mere customer, enjoy the view from my bedroom window. It is in the role of member of the public that I object to the great ugly pylon that has been planted among those otherwise unspoiled acres.

However, in the case of the pylon, I do not really rage about it because, after all, if it were not for those things I would be carrying in the coal each morning. At the same time I am still a little sensitive in my role of member of the public and attended a protest meeting held in the village hall the other day. It is generally true that the attitude of the 'public' towards a business is modified in those who as well as being public are customers or, better still, shareholders.

Public relations are often difficult for the management of businesses distributing their products to a small, select section of the community. For example, public opinion of vehicle constructors is often embittered by the sight of diesel lorries belching out black smoke for the sake of reduced costs for the haulage contractor. Similarly, firms who distribute large noisy motor-cycles to a small section of intrepid and thoughtless young men rarely escape public censure.

These are examples where distribution distinguishes the roles of customer and member of the public. It is possible for distribution to be so widespread that the two roles become blurred. For example, in the days when almost everyone travelled by rail at some time or another, some railway companies talked of public relations when they were referring to relations with passengers. But when it comes to the nuisances occasioned by

the process of production, the co-existence of customer enjoyment is often not sufficient to make the nuisance tolerable.
I doubt whether my enjoyment of the benefits of steel would
reconcile me to living next door to a steel mill. Probably only
those people who earn their living there would be willing to
suffer such dirt and ugliness intruding into their role as members
of the public.

Managers plainly wish to manipulate the attitude of the
public, to make them forget the nuisances caused by their
business and to make them appreciate more fully the value of
the product and the excellence of everything and everyone
concerned in its production. They do this sometimes to lessen
the chances of their business being interfered with in the
interests of the public, but more often to convert public into
customers.

The main channels through which they work today are the
press, radio, television and leaders of thought like teachers and
lawyers. The employment of specialist public-relations managers
is much more widespread than the employment of customer-
relations managers referred to in the last chapter. One such
specialist describes his job as one of finding out what the public
is thinking, to encourage opinion favourable to his business and
to change opinion that is hostile to his business. He also firmly
believes that it is sometimes necessary to probe deeply to get at
what the public really thinks, and for this reason the motiva-
tional research techniques pioneered by Dr Dichter are justifiable.

It is argued by others that the Public Relations Officer is
behaving in a similar way to the lawyer who argues a case for
his client and pleads a cause by putting the best possible light
on his client's actions. This professional position is claimed even
more readily by the principals of public relations agencies who
will act for any business that hires their services. Public relations agencies in some countries are rapidly overtaking
advertising agencies in numbers and prestige.

Much of the efforts of these specialists goes to securing what
they refer to as 'coverage' in press, radio and television. By
'coverage' they sometimes mean favourable comment, but some
argue that any mention is better than no mention at all. The
growing practice of giving 'hand-outs' to journalists is not
without its dangers to reputable reporting, and the public finds

it increasingly difficult to determine whether 'items of news' originate from a journalist or a public relations writer.

Unfortunately some managers now feel that they need to be accompanied by specialist press officers when they meet journalists to protect themselves from misrepresentation. This is a sad and, in many cases, unwarranted reflection on the activities of journalists. But the fact is that the press plays an important part in building public images of companies. Newspapers dealing predominantly with financial matters are particularly important, as through their influence on the price of shares, they may well influence the ability of a business to lay hands on fresh funds at a critical time.

CHAPTER IV

ORGANISATION AND
EXTERNAL RELATIONS

We have already seen how some businesses include in their organisation certain specialists in external relations. These specialists are usually of managerial rank and enjoy such titles as customer relations, passenger relations and public relations officers. They are like members of the Foreign Office in Government. The Foreign Office does not set itself up to be the only or the most important channel for the conduct of the country's external relations. It deals with a relatively small volume of particularly delicate matters that are referred to collectively as 'political'. In business, external relations departments are similarly largely concerned with a relatively small number of issues that involve 'policy'.

When is a matter one of policy and when is it not? The notion expressed by the term as it is used in industry is usually vague. Many managers talk of policy as anything that their superiors have given a ruling on. In this sense it has the nature of a standing order. At other times it is used to cover issues that are important to all branches of an organisation. These branches will probably have different viewpoints on issues that concern them all, so it is necessary to impose an official attitude to be taken in dealings with outsiders to avoid the dangers of equivocation. It is an important part of the work of the external relations experts to represent the official view of the business.

To put their role in perspective we must bear in mind the fact that the day to day problems of external relations are dealt with by managers in almost every part of an organisation. No amount of expertise can enable any manager to escape his personal responsibility for good external relations. Even though the sales manager may appear to shoulder a large share of responsibility in his concern for customer-relations, from what has been said it should be clear, for example, that the responsibilities of production managers and accountants, although less obvious, are no less important.

At the head of many business organisations there are two people, one responsible to the other, who may be called chairman and managing director, or chairman and chief executive. Their roles may be compared in some respects with that of sovereign or president, and prime minister. The former is head of State from the viewpoint of external relations and the latter boss of internal relations. It is the fact that only one person reports to the supreme authority that is puzzling in this organisation pattern.

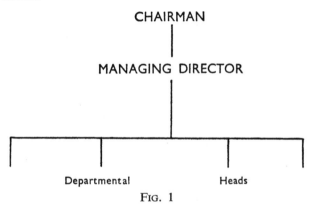

FIG. 1

But the device is seen to be logical if one of them is regarded primarily as outward looking and the other as inward looking. Inward and outward are used from the standpoint of the business organisation we are illustrating. This relationship may be pictured as shown in Fig. 2 on page 50.

If this picture is a true one, two things are happening. First the main pressures from external groups are exerted on the chairman and the main pressures from internal groups are exerted mainly on the managing director. Secondly, the image of the organisation presented to external groups is created by the chairman, and the image of the organisation presented to internal groups is created by the managing director.

The two men may in fact present the same face. This may result from a coincidence of views or the domination of one by the other. The dominant one is not always the chairman, who is sometimes a mere figurehead or 'front' man. But what if the two images are different?

Difficulties arise because the roles of chairman and managing director cannot be mutually exclusive. The chairman must have some say in internal relations and the managing director must

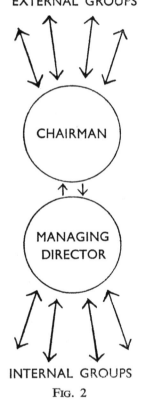

FIG. 2

have some influence on external relations. The two voices are bound to make life more difficult for those managers concerned with the day-to-day conduct of the business and its external relations.

I want now to take a closer look at the way outsiders criticise business organisations, and the reasons for their criticisms. I do not mean criticism of the finished product. This may be highly satisfactory and yet the business may provoke hostility through the way it is organised. For the moment the only thing we need note about organisation is that it involves a number of people, each of whom is doing only a part of the overall task, and that some of these people are more important than others. Some have more authority than others.

It sometimes happens that when an outsider asks a question of someone in a business the latter is unable to answer through lack of knowledge. He may then refer the outsider to someone else who cannot answer his question. And this may go on several times. The enquirer is passed from hand to hand and has to begin at the beginning of his story on each occasion. Then all too often the last straw comes when he is referred back to the very person who started the frustrating sequence who still denies all knowledge of the matter. To the enquirer this is a clear case of the right hand not knowing what the left is doing, and moreover as revealing a careless disregard of the consequences.

If the left hand of an organisation does not know what the right is doing, then it must make provision for enquiries to be fed into a brain that will bring the right limb into action. An efficient information centre in place of the usual switchboard unit is sometimes all that is needed.

Then there is another common failing springing from the character of organisation. An enquirer is put on to someone who is well aware of his problem and is able to discuss it intelligently, but who at the end of several minutes admits that he has not sufficient authority to do what is asked. The enquirer is then referred to someone more senior in the organisation who is presumed to have the necessary authority. I say presumed because there is always a chance that he may have to refer the enquirer to an even more senior person.

It is obviously desirable than an outsider should not be made to suffer by the refinement of levels of authority in organisation. But it is not easy to simplify the approaches for an enquirer. It might be helpful to make a rule that whoever first receives the enquiry takes it up to the right level of authority himself, tells the story told to him and then leaves the more senior person to talk directly with the enquirer. This involves the danger inherent in passing on stories, but at least the organisation is prepared with some knowledge in its second encounter with the outsider.

A third source of annoyance is where an enquirer obtains an 'authoritative' answer from someone, only to find later that someone else in the organisation has a different but equally 'authoritative' answer to his question. If organisation is equivocal then dealings with it must be perplexing. But an absence of doubt brings no comfort in the situation where an undertaking given to an outsider by a junior is rescinded by his superior on the grounds that the former had overstepped his authority.

Internal routines and procedures, so necessary in the eyes of people within an organisation, may appear wholly irrelevant to the needs of those without. The devious workings of organisation are poor excuse for the delays and other inconveniences they cause customer and community. All of us have probably, at some time or other, got caught up in the works of some large and impersonal organisation. You know you are being dealt with; people are obviously busy with your affairs, even rushing around doing something about them; but what? Nobody tells you what is happening and you wonder if they have forgotten what you really want. Nobody could remember that long.

A business that is badly organised for the handling of its external relationships is not necessarily one that suffers from poor staff morale. The mistakes I have described can be produced where employees are cheerful, enthusiastic and determined to please. Bad morale makes an additional impression on the outsider.

For example, an enquirer may be passed from one person to another, not just because of a lack of organised information service but because employees are given to 'passing the buck'. Employees may possess the necessary knowledge and authority to deal with an enquiry, but will not commit themselves to an opinion or decision for fear of the consequences of doing wrong. This attitude is usually accompanied by a readiness to grumble about the organisation in front of outsiders, further destroying their confidence.

The morale of the employees of a business can, on the other hand, create for external parties an image of willing service and purposefulness.

PART II

INTERNAL RELATIONS OF
MANAGEMENT

'It is a brutal truth about the world that the
whole everlasting business of keeping the
human race protected and clothed and fed
could not go on for twenty-four hours
without the vast legion of hard-bitten,
technically efficient, not over-sympathetic
men, and without the harsh processes of
discipline by which this legion is made.'
C. S. LEWIS

CHAPTER V

ELEMENTS OF ORGANISATION

Any business employing a number of people may be referred to as an organisation. The tacking of the word 'organisation' on to the word 'business' appears casual and indiscriminate. If I refer to a business organisation, or to an organisation, am I adding anything to the idea conveyed by simply using the word 'business'?

Probably if you had not known it already I would thereby reveal that I was not talking of a one-man business. But this is doing no more than making use of the obvious idea that you cannot have an organisation of just one person.

To take a more significant step in our thinking we need to ask ourselves this: if we have a business organisation of, say, ten men, can we remove the organisation and still be left with a business? If the ten men were window-cleaners organised as a window-cleaning firm, could they cease to be organised as a firm and yet carry on with the business of cleaning windows? It seems they could. So the idea behind 'organisation' does, in fact, add something to the idea behind 'business'.

The point is finally made when we consider that window-cleaning firms have various organisations; the same kind of business, but with different kinds of organisation. There are ways of doing business with organisation that differ from doing business without organisation.

In every-day use the word 'organisation' is commonly associated with descriptive words like orderly, harmonious, self-preserving and purposeful. Words with meanings opposite to these, like muddled, discordant, self-destructive and aimless, are used to describe lack of organisation. We must be careful that this habit of thinking does not lead us into wrong ideas about business organisation. It does not follow that more highly organised business is more orderly, harmonious and so on, or that less organisation must lead to muddle and discord.

The word organisation comes from a Latin root which means an 'instrument'; that is to say, something with which actions are performed. In some cases instruments are used for actions that could otherwise be performed unaided. For example, I may use a wheelbarrow to carry a hundredweight of potatoes that I could otherwise carry on my back. On the other hand some instruments are used for actions that could not be performed without their aid. There is much that can be seen with the aid of optical instruments, that could not been seen with the naked eye.

Business organisations are instruments. They are means to ends. They are used to perform actions. They are not ends in themselves. Every manager needs to keep reminding himself of this fact. It is all too easy to slip into accepting that organisations are ends in themselves. There is plenty of evidence of the tragic consequences of believing that maintaining the organisation of State is more important than promoting the well-being of the individuals, for which it should be instrumental. If we are more concerned with maintaining a particular form of business organisation than with the customers' needs, then we are on the road to a business-like totalitarianism.

A business organisation is a complicated instrument; it is more like a piano than a violin. In fact the comparison with a piano or a musical organ is helpful to an understanding of organisation.

Each string in a piano can produce a certain musical note, and will not produce any other note if the right things are done to it. Each part of a business organisation, be it human or otherwise, possesses certain qualities that the organisation needs. Each man or machine is capable of performing a certain task. The raw materials used can be transformed into the state in which they are wanted. Just as the note produced by a piano string can be fitted into notes produced by other strings, so the contribution of a part of organisation can be fitted into the contribution of other parts. The parts can be made to do some-

thing together in time or in place; or they can be made to do the
same things but in different places. All these arrangements have
a predetermined end in view, whether it be a tune or a motor-
car.

The pleasure that we get from a musical note is the result of a
change made in the state of a taut string. A string at rest is made
to move by a blow from a hammer that is itself moved by a key.
The satisfaction we get from knives and forks results from
changes made in the shape of metal by tools controlled by men.
The operatives in business may be likened to the keys in the
piano. And just as the keys of a piano are made to act in an
orderly way by a pianist, so the operatives of a business are
made to work in an orderly way by managers.

This analogy is illustrated by the diagram on page 58.

You are probably tired of this analogy by now, but I want to
pursue it further because there are still a few points that it can
help us with. Firstly each man intends to create something new
by the process of changing what is already there. In order to
begin, sustain and carry out this intention he needs to symbolise
what he is going to create by a plan. In each case his intention
can be viewed as something that is independent of his action to
carry out his intention. The action may or may not succeed in
achieving his intention. The action in each case is carried out
through an organisation that is instrumental in his purpose.

In each case, and in one sense at the far end of organisation,
there are *objects of change*. In business organisations producing
goods these are generally referred to as raw materials. In business
organisations producing services they are customers or clients.
From now on I shall refer to 'raw materials' because there
is no suitable short term to cover both materials and people
(i.e. passengers, clients, customers, etc.) who are objects of
change.

In the middle of each organisation we have *agents of change*.
These are the immediate and material instruments of change.
The blow of a hammer, the cutting of a chisel or the boring of
a drill are the crucial acts. In business the agents of change
are equipment in the widest sense, so that they may be chemical
plants, smelting plants, giant presses or garden hoes. They are
agents in the sense that they are directed by operatives.

In piano organisation and in business organisation there are
the third main elements, the *operatives*, that are keys in the one

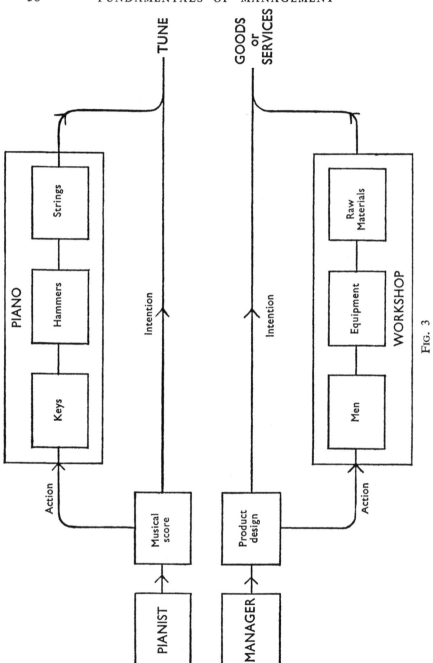

FIG. 3

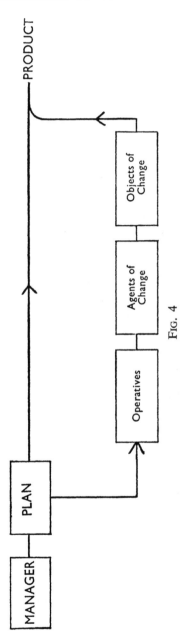

Fig. 4

case, and men in the other. So the basic elements of business organisation may be illustrated as shown in Fig. 4, page 59.

So far in the illustration I have linked the various parts of organisation by lines, without attaching much significance to the links. This is wrong. The links are very important.

But before dealing with the subject of the connections between parts of organisation I want to emphasise that so far I have shown the manager as standing outside his organisation. This is quite deliberate, although many managers are themselves contained within a larger organisation, every manager has his own organisation that is instrumental to his purpose. This is really what distinguishes a manager from other sorts of people in business, this acting *through an organisation*. And every business organisation has the three essential parts referred to above.

This analysis will enable us to avoid some of the dangers inherent in the definition of a manager as 'a man who acts through other people'. This is true, but so incomplete that it over-simplifies the organisational task of managers. The reasons for this should be more apparent from what follows.

The connections between the pianist and his piano, and among the various parts of the piano are fairly simple. The pianist must be able to understand and interpret the score, and then by direct physical movement depress the right keys. The keys are connected to the hammers by a simple rod and lever system. A simple movement connects hammer and string.

Likewise, the manager must thoroughly understand his plan and translate it from symbols to action. After this initial similarity of an ideas connection, the connections in business organisation become very much more complex than those in piano playing. The connection between manager and operative is the expression of ideas through words or other symbols; the connection between operative and equipment is the use of personal and variable skill. The connection between equipment and raw material is one of the equipment changing the material. But the degree of change alters according to the extent to which the material is responsive to a particular design of equipment. This may now be illustrated diagrammatically in Fig. 5.

The process of setting up any business organisation is, therefore, basically as follows:

1. Someone must furnish an idea of the product, whether it be

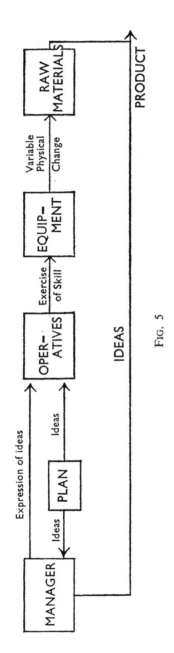

Fig. 5

goods or services. This someone is more often than not someone other than the manager.

2. The idea of the product must then be expressed in a plan that will capture the idea and analyse it into operational steps. The plan will then be a reservoir of ideas on which both manager and operatives may draw.

3. The manager must then assemble operatives, equipment and raw materials *that are able* to meet his needs. There is a wealth of meaning in the phrase 'that are able' because it embraces the critical decisions involved in matching capacity to needs. The needs must be estimated exactly, and capacity must be judged accurately.

4. Operatives, equipment and materials must then be arranged in the manner best suited to put the plan into action. 'Arrangement' consists essentially in locating, timing and connecting the various parts.

5. The organisation is then put into motion by the expression of ideas flowing from management in the form of instructions, advice and so on. Business organisations commonly fail in these ways:

(a) Where the initial idea of the product is bad, either quantitatively or qualitatively.

(b) Where a good initial idea is not well designed in detail. In these circumstances the inventor fails to get his ideas expressed in a form that will convey to other people exactly what he means.

(c) Where a manager fails through his own shortcomings to understand the design of a product.

(d) Where a manager fails to match operatives, equipment and materials to the specification of the product, quantitatively or qualitatively. This failure may be one of providing too much or too little capacity.

(e) When a manager fails through his own shortcomings to put over his ideas to operatives.

(f) Where operatives are incapable of understanding a clear expression of ideas by management.

(g) Where operatives are incapable of using equipment as it should be used.

(h) Where the raw materials used are not amenable to the action of the particular equipment used in the business.

CHAPTER VI

THEORY OF ORGANISATION

There are ways of doing business with organisation. There are ways of doing business without it. These statements were made in the last chapter, but the ideas were not pursued. We must now take a close look at them in order to produce a statement of the facts on which organisation depends. A complete explanation must include an examination of the alternative to organisation. The hypothesis proposed as explanation in this chapter is new, but it draws on some well-tried mental tools fashioned for us by economists.

All we have done so far is to pick out six elements of organisation and label them as follows:

1. expression of ideas (advice, instruction, orders, etc.),
2. operatives,
3. exercise of skill,
4. equipment,
5. physical change,
6. raw materials,

and to classify operatives, equipment and raw materials as *physical elements* and ideas, skill, and change as *link elements*. This set of labels may not by itself seem very useful, but some such are indispensable in an attempt to examine organisations systematically.

To illustrate some general principles I am going to refer to the business of a photographer. His particular intention is to obtain portrait and scenic photographs, and to sell them to the general public, magazines and the press. As it is a business he also intends that the total value of his sales will exceed his total costs by an amount big enough to give him a living. The label 'product' was given in the last chapter to what a business intends, but it must be understood to include selling the product. So that really the intention is to get *a return for a product* and not the product itself. This distinguishes a business organisation from the organisation involved in playing a piano for enjoyment only.

Some writers in pursuit of this line of thinking stress that the purpose of all businesses is to sell, or as Drucker has put it, 'to create a customer'. This is useful if it corrects the tendency of not thinking beyond the point of obtaining the product. But there is the danger of over-correction and of falling into the opposite error. Selling is the culminating act of business, in the sense that it is the last in a series of business acts, and it is the one that brings in the final reward. But it is wrong to ignore the fact that just as much care and attention has to be given to the way a product is obtained as to its sale.

Our photographer decides to begin business in this way. He will use his own savings to buy the equipment he needs and to keep himself until he can begin to draw on some returns to the business. He will sell only photographs that he has taken himself. He will do his own developing, printing, mounting and framing. He will buy his own raw materials, keep his accounts and sell his products from rented premises.

This one-man business is a fair success and leads the photographer to believe that he could sell many more photographs than he is able to produce on his own. To him it is basically a question of how to obtain more photos, and he could do it by producing more himself, if someone else took some of the other jobs off his hands, or by getting other people to produce photographs for him to sell.

Whatever he does his actions will fall into one of two categories. He will either undertake additional work by contract or undertake it by organisation.

He might decide to do his processing, selling and book-keeping by contract. After taking photos himself he would send them to a specialist developing and printing firm. He would then mount and frame the photos and send them to a selling agent to dispose of them. He would also get his books kept by a firm of accountants. All these steps would give him more time in which to take photographs.

Alternatively he may decide to do all the extra work by organisation. He might then employ a man to take photographs, another to process negatives and a third to act as salesman.

What are the essential differences in these two courses of action? In contracting he reduces the number of different kinds of tasks he has to perform, and probably reduces the equipment that he requires. Finally, he introduces someone between himself and the tools of the trade. In organisation he maintains or may even increase the number of different kinds of tasks he has to perform, and probably increases the equipment he requires. Again he introduces people between himself and the tools of the trade.

The first thing to note is that both courses involve getting things done through other people. In the one case he and the other people are drawn together by contract, and in the other case the other people are subordinated to him in authority. Getting things done through other people is not, as is often said, a peculiarity of organisation.

In organisation, business elements are related by subordination instead of by contract. Much of the strength of organisation is founded on the principles of subordination. From it spring many of the problems of organisation. Subordination may, on balance, produce great benefits, but every honest man must concern himself with the very important issues still lying on the lighter scale.

Our photographer might well find that it would 'pay' him personally to go along to a well-established photographic organisation and obtain a salaried position in the organisation. He would lose many of the satisfactions of free-lancing. He would probably no longer work with his own tools on his own materials. His main relationship with other people in business would change from the contractual relationship he previously enjoyed with his customers, to the organisational relationship in which he is subordinate.

The theory of organisation that I wish to propound in this chapter is an answer to the following four questions.

What causes a business man to 'organise' instead of 'contract'? What are the limits to the size of organisation? In what order does organisation occur, i.e. what activities are subordinated first? What determines the final proportion of physical elements (operatives, equipment and raw materials) and what effect does this proportion have on link elements?

C

A business man will generally choose to organise if he expects savings on the costs of contracting. The savings expected must be great enough to compensate him for the time and trouble it will take him to subordinate further elements. He will also consider any uncertainties in the alternatives. He may judge it imprudent to rely on a contractor for a small but vital process. Or he may not wish to run the risk of failure in the delivery of tools needed for a job.

The headaches of organisation are not viewed in the same way by all business men when it comes to weighing them against savings. Some men prefer empire for its own sake and are impatient of trading.

An organisation tends to grow to a point where its rate of production will give the maximum profit to be obtained *solely in organisation*. In the illustration on page 67 this is at stage 6 or 7 to produce a quantity of 6,000 or 7,000 at a profit of 8,400. This point is reached when marginal cost (the cost of the last unit produced) equals marginal sales value (the price at which the last unit can be sold). If the business can sell, without having to reduce the price, at whatever rate it chooses to produce, then contracting will not prevent organisation growing to the size it would have reached had contracting not been considered.

Let us continue to look at the situation illustrated. The rate of selling that will reap the highest profit is 12,000 to 13,000 a month, and if there is no shortage of capital this is the rate at which business should begin. Of the 12,000 to 13,000, 6,000 would be obtained by contracting and 6,000 to 7,000 would be produced by its own organisation. Any increase or decrease in the overall rate or change in the proportion obtained by the two methods would cause profits to diminish.

But because of shortage of capital, in fact, not all businesses are able to begin at optimum size. They have to begin with a low rate of production and increase it stage by stage. Let us assume the worst. Although our business man knows that a rate of 12,000 a month would maximise his profits, he cannot raise enough capital or obtain sufficient credit to begin with more than 1,000 a month.

If he is optimistic about his prospects of rapidly increasing his capital to enable him to produce at the rate of 5,000 a month, he may decide to obtain his first 1,000 by contracting. Thus he

PROFIT in Organisation	Costs in Organisation			Rate of production at each stage of Organisation			Costs in Contracting			PROFIT in Contracting
	Marginal cost per Unit	Average cost per unit of Production	Total Cost of Organisation	Stage	Rate in Units per Month	Sales Value	Cost of total Product	Average cost per unit of Production	Marginal cost per Unit	
1200	3·8	3·8	3800	1	1000	5000	4000	4	4	1000
2800	3·4	3·6	7200	2	2000	10000	7800	3·9	3·8	2200
4800	3·0	3·4	10200	3	3000	15000	11100	3·7	3·3	3900
7200	2·6	3·2	12800	4	4000	20000	13600	3·4	2·5	6400
8000	4·2	3·4	17000	5	5000	25000	15000	3·0	1·4	10000
8400	4·6	3·6	21600	6	6000	30000	18000	3·0	3·0	12000
8400	5·0	3·8	26600	7	7000	35000	23800	3·4	5·8	11200
6400	7·0	4·2	33600	8	8000	40000	31200	3·9	7·4	8800
3600	7·8	4·6	41400	9	9000	45000	40500	4·5	9·3	4500
NIL	8·6	5·0	50000	10	10000	50000	52000	5·2	11·5	—2000

Illustration of possible differences in the costs of organisation and contracting at increasing rates of production. Selling price has been assumed to remain at a constant 5 per unit.

FIG. 6

will avoid saddling himself with the organisation that might stand in the way of his maximising profits in contracting. Organisations cannot be disbanded as readily as they are set up.

On the other hand, this course would mean a sacrifice of profit of 200 per month. He might well decide that he cannot afford this and that he will begin with organisation. Then if he has to grow slowly, stage by stage, he will next decide to step up to 2,000 a month. He is then faced with this situation. By obtaining the additional 1,000 by contracting, his costs would be 3,800 and 4,000 against a selling price of 10,000, giving a profit of 2,200. He might as well never have organised, as this is the profit he would make by contracting the lot, and now he would be losing 600 a month. So he decides on 2nd stage organisation.

When it comes to considering raising the rate of production to 3,000 per month we have to compare third stage organisational costs of 10,200 against second stage organisational costs of 7,200, plus first 1,000 contracting costs of 4,000.

Having set up the organisation the size will tend to grow, until the *marginal cost* under organisation exceeds the marginal contracting cost (i.e. at the lowest rate of production). In the situation illustrated this would mean that after the fourth stage of organisation the business would switch to contracting. After building up to 10,000 per month (i.e. 4,000 from organisation and 6,000 from contracting) it would revert to adding to its organisation two stages to obtain the extra 2,000 to maximise profits.

Two things remain to be said. The growth of organisation can be stopped at any point by shortage of capital. It might be stopped any time before reaching optimum size. Secondly, if the rate of production begins to affect price it could happen that organisation would not grow beyond a point at which a switch to contracting first occurred. For example, if it were necessary to reduce the price to 4 per unit in order to sell over 10,000 per month, organisation would not grow to a point where its rate of production will give the maximum profit to be obtained *solely in organisation*.

The third question we have to consider in a theory of organisation is the order in which activities are subordinated in organisation. We will continue with the illustration of the photographer who decides he could sell more than he is at present producing as a one-man business, and that by selling more he will increase his profit. We will assume that he has considered the alternative of contracting and has concluded that it would pay him to expand by creating an organisation. He has not much capital so must expand slowly. Which of the various activities in his business shall he organise first? The main ones are photographing, processing and selling. If he is going to employ only one assistant, in which of these fields shall it be?

He finds a man who can be employed in any of the three activities, but who naturally is not equally good at all three jobs. Shall he employ the man in the activity that he does best? The problem is illustrated below. The numbers of 'x' indicate the degree of skill in each activity. One degree of skill in any one activity is equally valuable to the business as one degree of skill in any other activity. It is assumed that if the employer had all the jobs to do himself he would do best to devote one-third of his time and skill to each activity, and if he had only two he would devote half to each.

	Photographing	Processing	Selling
Employer	$8x$	$2x$	$5x$
Employee	$4x$	$5x$	$6x$

FIG. 7

Working by himself the employer can employ $5x$ of skill [i.e. one-third $(8x + 2x + 5x)$]. If the employee does the processing he can employ $11.5x$ of skill [i.e. $\frac{1}{2}(8x + 5x) + 5x$]. If the employee does the photographing the result would be $7.5x$; if the employee does the selling the result would be $11x$.

This illustrates the general principle that an employer should first subordinate to organisation that activity in which he has the greatest disadvantage or least advantage. This does not necessarily mean that he should subordinate the activity that he is worst at, as the following example will show.

	Photographing	Processing	Selling
Employer	$9x$	$6x$	$4x$
Employee	$8x$	$2x$	$2x$

FIG. 8

It will pay him in this situation to subordinate the activity he is best at. The determining factor is the difference between his skill and his employee's skill in each activity. He has an advantage of x in photographing, $4x$ in processing and $2x$ in selling. He has the least advantage in photographing, and should, therefore, subordinate it first.[1] Notice that the principle still holds where the employer is better than the employee in all three activities.

We have already seen from the former of these two illustrations that it is not necessarily advantageous to get an employee to do the job he is best at. To this we must add that it is not necessarily advantageous for an employer to shed the job he is worst at.

The last part of this theory of organisation concerns the proportions in which the physical elements are found. What determines the proportions of men, tools and materials in organisation?

The physical elements of organisation will be combined together in such proportions that a reduction in the proportion of one element and consequent increase in another will bring about an increase in average costs. For such proportions the marginal costs of each element will be equal.

While this may be theoretically sound, how do we determine what proportion physical elements are in? It sounds easy, but it is not. The first difficulty is in finding a common basis for comparing operatives, equipment and raw materials.

The only possible measure appears to be that of the money-cost of using each element in producing and selling a given quantity of the product. Let us assume we found a business with these costs for each 1,000 units of product.

Operatives' wages	£1,000
Use of equipment	100
Buying of raw materials	700
Processing of raw materials under contract	1,200
Selling of product through agents	500
	£3,500

[1] It is, of course, possible to devise situations in which there is no *least* advantage or *greatest* disadvantage, and where it is a matter of indifference between two alternatives.

We might say that we have established the proportion of elements in organisation as 10 : 1 : 7, the remaining costs being those of contracting. But a moment's thought will reveal that the figure of £700 for raw materials is unsatisfactory. The cost of raw materials must reflect the amount of work done on the materials. The processing costs of £1,200 might well have been incurred before delivery of the materials, and included in a single charge of £1,900. The proportions would then have been 10 : 1 : 19 with no fundamental change in the organisational situation.

This becomes clearer if we look at what happens when the business decides to do the processing itself. We will assume that it still costs £1,200 in organisation.

Operatives' wages	£1,900
Use of equipment	400
Buying raw materials	700
Selling of product through agents	500
	£3,500

If contract processing charges are regarded as *preparation* costs for raw materials then agency selling costs may be regarded as *finishing* costs. Both costs can then be added to the buying price of materials to give us *true raw material costs*. This makes sense. Raw material is raw to the extent that it is unfinished for the purpose of selling. We can now say:

1. The true costs of raw materials reflect the costs of preparing and finishing outside of organisation.
2. The costs of operatives and equipment reflect the extent to which raw materials are unfinished for selling.
3. Another way of looking at this is that costs of operatives and equipment indicate extent to which work is carried out in organisation, and true cost of raw materials indicates extent to which work is carried out by contracting.
4. As organisation is increased the costs of operatives and equipment rise proportionately.
5. As organisation is decreased the true costs of raw materials rise proportionately.
6. The degree of organisation is indicated by the proportions of the physical elements of organisation.

CHAPTER VII

COSTS AND SAVINGS
OF ORGANISATION

Costs can tell us something about organisation. But it is very easy to mistake what they tell.

First, the sum of money spent on using operatives and equipment does not *by itself* show how much organisation there is. Only when this amount is compared with that spent on the use of raw materials can we draw conclusions on the extent of organisation. One way of looking at it is that the measuring begins with a statement of money values and ends with a simple expression of ratio. The proportions of physical elements, measured by the money spent on their use, indicate that a business is more or less highly organised than another business.

The money spent on the use of physical elements does not represent the full bill for organisation. Money has to be spent on the link elements. It costs money to pass information, set up checking and correction procedures, to adjust skills when needs change, and so on.

Lastly, organisation costs are not costs in the sense that they represent how much extra one has to pay for having organisation. Organisation costs are one of two main alternative ways of spending money. If the right decision has been made it is the alternative that will, in fact, save money, because the other alternative is more costly.

The next question is how is money really spent in the alternative of contracting? We have already found that there is a close relationship between what are normally regarded as contracting costs and the cost of raw materials. The latter includes the former. Contracting costs of the production processing sort appear separately only because they are for work done on raw materials after they have been bought.

Charges for the same sort of work done earlier would simply be included in the price of the raw materials.

By contracting a business may buy-in three things: 'producers' goods' (which are goods only partly finished), labour services and organisation services. Producers' goods are more likely than not to have been partly finished through the instrument of another firm's organisation. The contribution of labour services from one-man businesses is likely to be small. So contracting costs usually turn out to be money spent on another firm's organisation instead of one's own.

Why does a business choose to spend money on another organisation rather than on its own? The obvious answer is that the other organisation is cheaper than its own. But how can this be? Leaving aside the possibility of differences in the ability of managers, which would affect how well the organisation was used, what is there to make a difference between one organisation and another?

In a way organisations are like the human beings who work in them. The most significant differences in the performances of members of the human race lie less in their endowments at the peak of their powers than in the stages of their individual development. The differences in the performance of two men of the same age are generally not so great as the differences between a baby and a middle-aged man, and a middle-aged man and a very old man. So it is with organisations. Their performances, measured in terms of costs per unit of production, vary with their stage of development. The pattern of variations is not always similar to that of human development, but it is so in a surprisingly large number of firms.

The age of organisations is not measured in years and months, but in quantity of product per period of time. One thing to remember, however, is that an organisation can be planned to begin at any rate of production!

The resemblance between human life and business organisation may be used to illustrate another point. One of the important things about a child is that its powers are increasing year by year. One of the important things about later life is that at some points both physical and mental powers begin to diminish. The pattern in a business organisation might well be something like this. Between certain rates of output, say 1 to 250 units of output per day, the cost of producing each

c*

successive unit (usually referred to as the marginal cost) may decrease. The organisation gets more effective, step by step, over this range. Between other rates, say 251 to 500 units per day, the cost of producing each successive unit may not change. The marginal costs are constant. And again over a certain rate, say 500 a day, the marginal costs may rise. So we get the three stages of falling, constant and rising costs. The graph of progress would then look like Fig. 9 on page 75.

It is easy to see that if a firm is just beginning business, with this cost curve in front of it, and it wants only a small quantity of output, it must look around before deciding what to do. If there is another firm whose output is already high enough to have brought it to the beginning of the constant costs range, then it may pay the new business to deal with the old one. Even if the other firm were setting up business at the same time, but at the higher rate of production, it might still pay the one with the lower rate to forgo setting up its own organisation. I have said 'might' pay quite deliberately. Much would depend upon prospects. If the first business thinks that it is likely that they would need to raise this rate of output to 250 a day in a short time, then the situation is different. The one firm can look forward to a period of falling costs and the other to a period of rising costs. The present advantageous position of the one will be reversed in the future. It is rather like the man in his prime who now enjoys his superiority over the stripling, but knows that time will inexorably reverse it.

It is the fact of variable costs, and the fact that firms are in different stages of development, as seen by their different positions on a cost curve, that create the possibilities of profiting from the alternatives of organisation and contracting.

Having said this we should dispose of any doubts about whether or not the production costs of businesses regulate the contract price of services to other firms. We must distinguish here between the influences at work in consumers' markets, and the influences at work in the transactions among businesses. Some producers' goods, or raw materials, have a market price in the sense that they may be bought at a rate prevailing over a wide area, irrespective of differing average costs of production. If we ignore transport costs, coal, steel, and timber are this sort. Other producers' goods are so specialised to the customer that

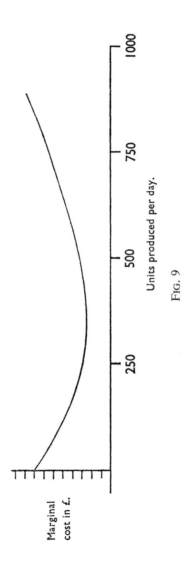

Fig. 9

there is no real market for them. Organisational services very often have no market price.

If one firm goes to another firm to get a job done, it usually needs something quite special to itself. There will not be a great number of buyers for this particular service, nor perhaps many sellers, so that market conditions do not exist. In fact, for these transactions between one firm and another prices are usually quoted on request. Organisational services are not so often advertised at a standard rate.

Why do the marginal costs of an organisation vary at all? What are the processes in organisation that may be compared with the physiological processes of growth and decay?

Marginal costs may fall because specialisation for the first time, and then increasing doses of it, is reducing costs. Organisation enables specialisation to occur because organisation brings men and tools and raw materials together. Then by arranging them in orders and suborders to suppress the unwanted, specialisation may emerge. In a less prosaic way Adam Smith says:

'A very trifling manufacture; but one in which the division of labour has been very often taken notice of, the trade of the pin-maker; a workman not educated to this business (which the division of labour has rendered a distinct trade), not acquainted with the use of the machinery employed in it (to the invention of which the same division of labour has probably given occasion), could scarce, perhaps, with his utmost industry, make one pin a day, and certainly could not make twenty. But in the way in which this business is now carried on, not only the whole work is a number of branches of which the greater part are likewise peculiar trades. One man draws out the wire, another straightens it, a third cuts it, a fourth points it, a fifth grinds it at the top for receiving the head; to put it on is a peculiar business, to whiten the pins is another; it is even a trade by itself, to put them into the paper; and the important business of making a pin is in this manner, divided into about eighteen distinct operations, which, in some manufactories, are all performed by distinct hands, though in others the same man will sometimes perform two or three of them. I have seen a small manufactory of this kind where ten men only were employed and where some of them consequently performed two or three distinct operations, and therefore but indifferently accommodated with the necessary machinery, they could, when they exerted themselves, make among them about twelve pounds of pins in a day. There are in a pound upwards of four thousand pins of a middling size. Those ten persons, therefore, making a tenth part of forty-eight thousand pins, might be considered as making four thousand eight hundred pins in a day. But if they had all wrought separately and independently, and without any of them having been educated to this peculiar business, they certainly could not each of them have made twenty, perhaps not one pin in a day; that is, certainly, not the two hundred and fortieth, perhaps not the four thousand eight hundredth part of what they are at present capable of performing, in consequence of a *proper division and combination* of their different operations.' (My italics.)

Adam Smith uses the term division of labour where we would nowadays more usually refer to specialisation.

The advantages of specialisation were illustrated in the last chapter in discussing the order in which skills are subordinated. Here is a simpler example, involving only two jobs, or specialisations.

Suppose two potters are making and selling the same jugs. The first one takes a day to make and two days to sell five jugs. The second takes a day-and-a-half to make and one day to sell five jugs. Working on their own the potters make and sell at the combined rate of three-and-two-thirds jugs a day. If they organise themselves to specialise by the first potter making jugs and the second selling them, their combined output will be five jugs a day.

Specialisation makes it possible to take advantage of differences in human endowments, dispositions and training. Because a specialist does not have so many different kinds of work to do he usually does not require such a great variety of tools as does a general worker. This makes for economies in the use of tools. Raw materials can be subjected to the particular skills they require and the particular tools that are most economic.

It is not unusual to find at some stages in its development that an organisation could produce at a higher rate than it is doing. There are a number of possible reasons. It might have been necessary to buy plant of a certain size, although something smaller would have done, just because there was no smaller plant to be had. Even the smallest farm tractor may be too large for the farmer with half an acre of land. Sometimes a business man buys some equipment that is more than he needs at the moment, because he believes demand for his product will grow and he does not want to change equipment too soon. Shipowners sometimes do this because anyway the costs of running a ship are not commensurate with the size of a ship. Running costs are not doubled by doubling the size of the vessel.

In situations where competition is imperfect, either because there is near-monopoly, or because of a price-fixing arrangement, a decrease in demand may result in many firms working below capacity. But whatever the cause, marginal costs will decrease as such a business increases its rate of production to the point where all the physical elements are fully used.

Finally, as the rate of production rises it becomes possible to install larger and more efficient machinery that would not be economic at a lower rate.

Marginal costs rise for two main reasons. Firstly, as the size of an organisation increases to handle higher rates of production, the difficulties of linking the various elements grow disproportionately. This is simply illustrated by showing diagrammatically the difference in linkage for 4 men and 8 men.

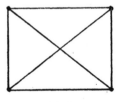

6 links

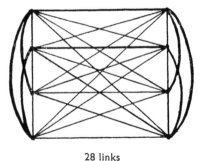

28 links

FIG. 10

Links rise according to the formula $(n-1)+(n-2)+(n-3)$ ... $n-(n-1)$, where 'n' = no. of physical elements. The searching for the right links becomes a more and more lengthy procedure. Ideas have a longer distance to travel and through more and more interchange points. We shall see more of these difficulties in the next chapter.

Finally, as organisations grow in size to raise their rate of production they may run into local scarcities in men and materials, and may be forced to obtain them from farther afield at greater cost because of the increased costs of transport. This would be one reason for a firm experiencing rising marginal costs.

CHAPTER VIII

PRINCIPLES OF SUBORDINATION

Organisation does not exist without superior and subordinate. It is true that crowds of men will sometimes act together without being led. In these exceptional cases it is usually a powerful instinct that compels each one to act in a certain way. But these irrational forces are as temporary as they are violent, and as unreliable as they are impressive.

Although we are all familiar with the relationship of superior and subordinate we seldom stop to give it much thought. Which is a pity. It is a relationship that gives rise to more bitterness than that of man and his proverbial mother-in-law. And all too often it is because we do not quite know what we have let ourselves in for when we take on the business of being a subordinate, or superior. All those in a subordinate position must face up to the unpleasant fact that organisation inevitably means some suppression of the will of the individual. On the other hand the benefits of organisation flow from this peculiar arrangement. A weak superior is often one who refuses to undertake the unpopular task of suppressing individual ideas.

The trouble is that it is not always easy to see the advantages that do come from suppression. The perplexity of human beings on this issue has made them swing throughout history from one doctrine to another. To this day in the political arena men are divided by their beliefs in tighter controls and less controls, in dictatorship and democracy.

Someone or something that is subordinate is regarded as being of a lower rank or order, and someone or something that is superior is regarded as being of higher rank or order. There is an idea of one being 'above' and one being 'below'. It is an idea that persists throughout human history, and, for all I know, prehistory. It probably originates in the belief that our destinies are controlled from the skies. We still cling to this up and down idea in drawing organisation charts, although some bold spirits have depicted organisation as circles, with the head-man in the centre. Perhaps these men have been more influenced by studies of beehives than the hierarchical structure of powers and principalities, angels and archangels.

Whatever mental pictures we use to help us understand the relationships we should be able to put some more precise ideas into words if we are to have our reasons accept the awkward features of organisation. A superior is someone of greater status, that is to say standing, in the organisation. A man can have greater status for a whole variety of reasons. A superior does not have to be superior to his subordinates in physical strength, mental ability, character and so on. Organisational standing may be related quite aptly to age, experience, or even family. It is, of course, important to sort out what it should be related to, and then to suppress irrelevant claims to higher status.

A subordinate is one who is controlled, who is dependent, and who is obliged to render certain services to his superior. A superior's right to control is called his authority. Authority is variable in that it may be great or little. Authority includes the idea of the role of an author. It implies originating and giving existence to things and situations. A man with authority is one who gives rise to actions.

A subordinate's dependence is indicated by the need for his superior's permission to act. A subordinate carries out his duties by commission or by permission. His obligations to render certain services to his superior are known as his responsibilities.

Men have always concerned themselves with the question of where authority comes from. There have been centuries of conflict involving views on the derivation of Kings' rights of control over their subjects. For a long time, in England, government was based on the theory that the King's authority was Divine as it came directly from God. The consequences of assuming the Divine Right of Kings were very important indeed to the organisation of State.

The consequences of abandoning this theory in favour of Constitutional Monarchy were far-reaching too. This new idea was that the King got his authority from a constitution. He

derived it from the agreement implicit in setting up the organisation of State. The monarch remained, as he had been for centuries, the fount of all authority. But there was a big difference.
He received that authority not from God, who was outside the
organisation, but from political organisation itself. So authority
could no longer be considered absolute. It was limited by the
laws of State, that the King helped to make. It was exercised
within the conditions of a form of social contract, and there it
remains, in England to this day.

Ideas on the source of industrial authority have played an
equally important part in the history of industrial organisation.
At one extreme we have the nineteenth-century ideas of the
'absolute' right derived from the ownership of capital. This
divine right enabled owner-managers to hire and fire employees
without question or other perceptible twinges of the social
conscience. It was at the root of the belief that challenges in any
shape or form to industrial authority should be regarded as
criminal, and as treasonable affronts to the authority of State.
No one can deny that there were fearful abuses of this absolute
power.

When Acton spoke of the corrupting influence of power he
was, of course, referring to political power. When ordinary,
decent men come into power, that power changes them for the
worse, and where power is absolute they end up wholly evil.
In twentieth-century industrial management there are formid-
able curbs to authority. There is even talk of the desirability of
elected management. But there is still plenty of evidence of the
difficulty in checking men in business who claim they must have
'complete control' in order to do their job.

The size of some industrial organisations considered alongside the phenomenon of their not having an owner to whom
management is responsible has caused many people to wonder if
the authority of the men at the top is virtually absolute and thus
totally corrupting. Anthony Sampson, in an article in *The
Observer*, January 22, 1961: Week End Review, p. 25, says:

'... many economists, even quite radical ones, have been
surprised to discover that these corporations behave better,
and more in the public interest, than they had expected. Several
explanations have been offered as to why big business has not
proved so menacing as it might be; the development of a

managerial class, concerned with prestige as much as profits; the competing pressures of specialist departments; the growth of "countervailing power" from trade unions or retailers; or the emergence of a "corporate" conscience.'

What are the bases for industrial authority today? There are still sections of industry, particularly in agriculture, and family manufacturing businesses, where authority is still closely related to social rank and privileges. Such authority appears patronising and responsible. It may be found to be surprisingly acceptable to workpeople, who do not find it oppressive. And it is often very effective management.

All too often the situation is that management authority is based precariously on the self-interest of the employees. As long as employees have the feeling that they are doing all right they will obey, or, as they prefer to say, co-operate with management. As soon as they see they have more to gain by challenging the authority of management, they do so. Joint consultation and other enlightened personnel practices seem to have little effect on the situation.

This is the dilemma of industrial organisation. It must maintain the authority of *selected* leaders in a society dedicated to upholding the political principles of *elected* leadership. It must maintain authority that is not met half-way by acceptance of moral obligations. There is very little to cling to in ideas on how to be a good leader or a good follower.

In this sort of climate we must turn to the institution of law that still commands great respect from the average citizen. Management authority should be based on the law of the land. It should spring from the contractual obligations inherent in the relationship of employer and employee. A manager's right to control should be a right to give lawful commands necessary for the proper conduct of business. And it should not go beyond this.

The employee's obligations should be more clearly legal obligations. He should be restrained by the duty to obey lawful commands while he is under contract. In other words, he should be required to give reasonable notice to escape his contractual obligations. Management's right to control would, of course, be matched by legal obligations to abide by an agreement on conditions of service for the employee. Just as the employee's obligations would be matched by rights to fair treatment from his employer.

And now we must consider what happens to authority after it leaves its source. Authority can be passed on. But it cannot be given away in the sense that if I pass on half my authority I am left with only half of it. I still have all of my authority, while the other man has half of it. We can illustrate this simply if we confine our thinking for the moment to authority over men. Let us assume an organisation of a hundred operatives and measure authority in terms of numbers of operatives controlled; the picture may look like Fig. 11 on page 85.

Numbers in boxes show numbers of men controlled. Although he has delegated all his authority the top man can still make decisions to control 100 operatives. Although each manager in the 2nd rank has delegated all his authority, he can still make decisions to control 20 operatives. We have a three-hundred men control, one hundred contained in each layer of authority. Looked at another way, 3 authorities bear upon each group of 10 men. One way of expressing weight of authority in a whole organisation would be in terms of the ratio of control power to numbers controlled, in this case 300 : 100.

The weight of authority bearing on a single section can be expressed as a ratio of number of authorities to numbers of men, in this case 3 : 10

Another way of looking at the distribution of authority in an organisation is to look at the spending power of individuals. This is often limited by budgeting for a maximum expenditure over a trading period, and additionally by laying down a maximum sum for any single outlay. This is an ill-defined situation that may give rise to anomalies (Fig. 12).

The spending power of the 2nd rank exceeds that of the 1st rank at any moment of time. This is not quite as significant as it looks at first sight as, of course, we are comparing power to spend on one single item with power to spend on three single items. These illustrations over-simplify, but they may be useful in suggesting approaches to the problem of assessing the distribution of authority in organisation.

In recent years there has been much loose thinking on the subject of delegation of authority. Many leaders of opinion have been encouraging more extensive delegation in business management. We cannot doubt their good intentions, but the

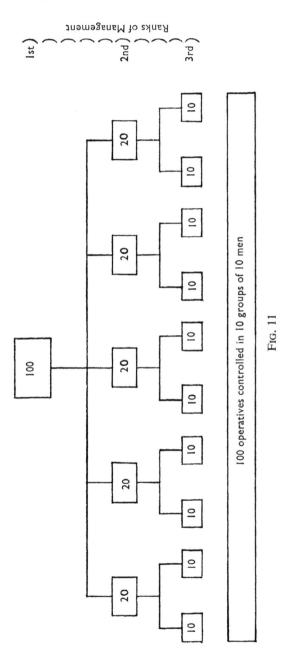

Ranks of Management

1st   2nd   3rd

100 operatives controlled in 10 groups of 10 men

Fig. 11

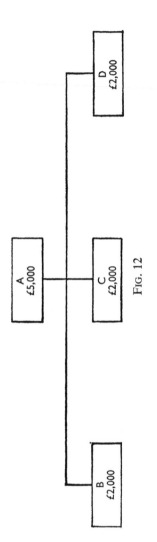

Fig. 12

influence of their teaching can be disastrous. Some advocate what they refer to as 'democratic' leadership, and oppose what they refer to as 'authoritarian' leadership. By this they usually mean that authority in business should not be concentrated in the hands of a single man, or even a few men. Authority should be distributed as widely as possible. By this means there is more initiative in the whole organisation.

These ideals have two serious flaws. They belittle the dangers of adding to the weight of authority in an organisation. Additions to weight of authority very probably add to the tasks of subordinates. They must suffer more control. T. E. Lawrence tells vividly of his misery at the Uxbridge RAF depot at a time when there were more NCOs than aircraftsmen. Secondly, these ideals obscure the truth that authority cannot be delegated without creating more authority, and that among human beings the fresh authority is quite likely to be used *against* its originator. The root of frequent purges in totalitarian regimes lies in the enormous power that is delegated to individuals, not in its concentration in the hands of the dictator. Dictators are soon frightened by the authority they have given to subordinates.

In democratic societies, once power has been passed on to lower ranks the situation is often irretrievable. The President of the USA is a prisoner in his own organisation. This may be good politics, but it is bad business.

There is a widely accepted principle that you can delegate authority, but cannot delegate responsibility. I do not think that it makes any sense. It is true that a subordinate's obligations to perform certain services for his superior cannot be given away. But, as we have already seen, neither can authority be given away. A subordinate can, however, impose obligations upon his own subordinates to help him fulfil those he owes to his superior. So just as the weight of authority in an organisation can be added to, so can the weight of responsibility be added to. There is really no difference between authority and responsibility from the point of view of passing them on.

Another principle of doubtful value is that 'the extent of a manager's authority should be determined by his responsibility'. Many extensive responsibilities do not need authority to carry them out. They may require permission from above. But authority should not be used as a synonym for permission. For example, you may have permission to leave the office at

4 o'clock, but you have not the authority to permit others to leave at that time. Authority initiates and does not refer merely to a state of being permitted. Authority is over other people and things. Permission is from other people.

Finally, if the *basis* for managerial authority were the law, would this adequately define its limits? The definition of authority as 'a right to give lawful commands necessary for a proper conduct of business' goes some way to setting limits. Authority must not be used to commit or cause to be committed any unlawful act. But the question of what is necessary for the proper conduct of business must leave much room for individual discretion.

Some people argue that a manager's authority must be confined to strictly economic situations, and should not extend to wider social fields. They are critical of those firms who concern themselves with staff welfare schemes such as housing, sports clubs, education and so on. They are even more critical of firms who provide amenities to the general public, for example, educational endowments, and patronage of the arts.

But it is impossible to confine the responsibilities of all managers to the strictly economic. We have already seen that in his external relations a manager must take positive steps to avoid making his business a public nuisance. He may have to exercise his authority to enforce conduct that is un-economic to the business. Again there are some undertakings, particularly transport, where managers' authority must be exercised to ensure the safety of customers and general public. All this means that the limits of managerial authority cannot be rigidly defined.

CHAPTER IX

ORGANISATIONAL GROUPS

A good organiser is one who successfully subordinates men, equipment and materials to his own purpose. His success will depend very much on the way he divides and connects up again. Physical elements must first of all be grouped; that is, collected into a number of unities that are distinct from other unities. Then the groups must be linked by authority to ensure their co-operation.

The unities and distinctions inherent in the nature of the three elements compel a basic pattern on any organisation. Operatives, equipment and materials have to be separately provided. They are usually brought into organisation by different routes (although we still cling to the practice of recruiting craftsmen *and* their tools), and then accommodated separately for at least part of the time. But most organisations contain some subdivision of these natural divisions. The alternatives are these:

   (i) to divide operatives into groups and leave equipment and materials undivided,

  (ii) to divide equipment into groups and leave operatives and materials undivided,

 (iii) to divide materials into groups and leave operatives and equipment undivided,

 (iv) to divide both operatives and equipment into groups and leave materials undivided,

  (v) to divide operatives and materials into groups and leave equipment undivided,

 (vi) to divide equipment and materials into groups and leave operatives undivided,

(vii) to divide operatives, equipment and materials into groups.

We will now look at each of these separately and with the aid of diagrams. The symbol 'o' stands for operative, 'e' for equipment, and 'm' for raw materials. Different types of equipment and raw materials are indicated in this way: $e, e^1, e^2, \ldots m, m^1, m^2, \ldots$

There are relatively few forms of activity in which only operatives are grouped. The situation presupposes either a number of identical tools, probably of a simple nature, or a big piece of machinery that is indivisible. All operatives on duty

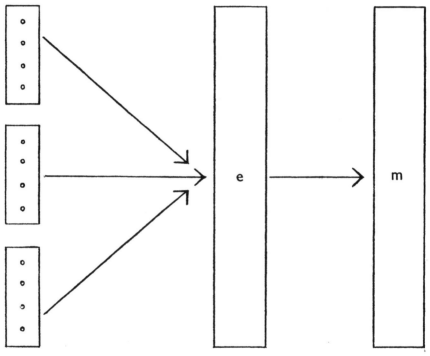

FIG. 13

at any one time are using all available equipment on all available material at any one time. The operatives are likely to be grouped for one of two reasons. Twelve operatives working together may prove to be unmanageable, as they cannot be watched closely enough. So they are split into three groups of four men, with a supervisor for each group. This might happen in some simple construction jobs like road building, where men work in small gangs under a ganger and where tools are very simple. Otherwise operatives may be grouped in this way so that work can go on throughout the twenty-four hours of a day. For example, three gangs of four stokers may man a furnace on a three-shift system over five days a week.

So far then we have found two bases for grouping operatives. One is a numerical basis—to reduce numbers of men in a group to a manageable size. The other is a time basis, when men are put in a number of groups to cover a period that is longer than can be worked by one group. And we have established two reasons why equipment is sometimes not grouped. Firstly, tools may be so uniform and simple that it is pointless to group them. Secondly, some forms of equipment are indivisible. They require a certain number of men to operate them, and that is that.

Again, it is unusual to find activities in which only equipment is grouped. In the situation illustrated below all the operatives use each of the three types of equipment in turn. Men are not allocated to a particular type of equipment. The raw material is of uniform nature or character throughout and is processed in three stages by the three types of equipment.

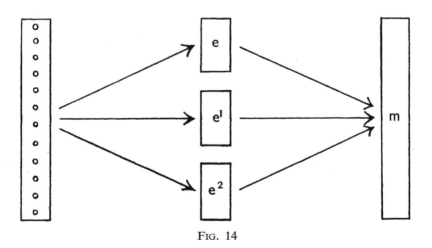

FIG. 14

These conditions are found in agriculture. The lifting, carting and stacking of crops is an illustration. The operatives are not divided because it is fairly easy for them to master the use of all the equipment which is of a simple nature, also the task is such

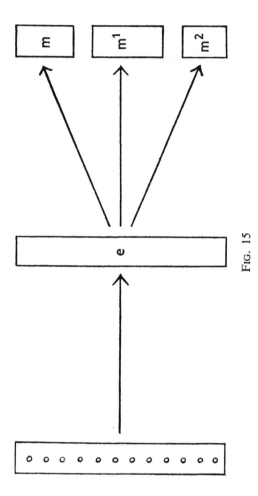

FIG. 15

that they do not need close supervision. Then, because of the need for the processes to be consecutive, allocation of men to each sort of equipment would cause two-thirds of the men to be idle at any one time. The process cannot be continuous because of the seasonal supply of the raw material.

Equipment is grouped here because each type is specialised to a process. Materials are ungrouped because of homogeneity.

The grouping of raw materials for operatives and equipment that remain undivided is a more common situation than the previous two (Fig. 15).

Firstly, the raw materials may be batched for ease of handling. For example, in large accounting departments customers' records may be handled in alphabetically separated sections. Secondly, batches of materials may differ in character and require different applications of the same tool. For example, different sorts of documents may have to be collected together for separate processing in a computer. Thirdly, geographical separation of units of raw material give rise to a natural grouping. Gangs of bricklayers moving from one site to another is an example. Lastly, where occupations are seasonal, like fishing, there is a natural material grouping.

It is not until we group two of the three organisational elements that we get specialisation. If operatives and equipment are grouped then we get specialisation in equipment use (Fig. 16).

In this situation it is unlikely that all three groups of men will be able to work on all the material at any one time. In most cases the jobs done by particular pieces of equipment must be done in a certain order. This would leave men and equipment idle unless fresh raw material was being fed in continuously to go through each process in turn.

Similarly, by the grouping of operatives and raw materials we can obtain specialisation in types of raw material (Fig. 17).

For example, if the twelve operatives were tailors, each of three groups might be required to deal with particular grades or types of cloth. This situation requires operatives who are generally skilled in their trade, and are accustomed to the use of a complete range of equipment. It is a form of specialisation that enables an operative to get to know the peculiarities of particular materials and the consequent need for changes in methods of using equipment.

Next we have a grouping based on the need to use special

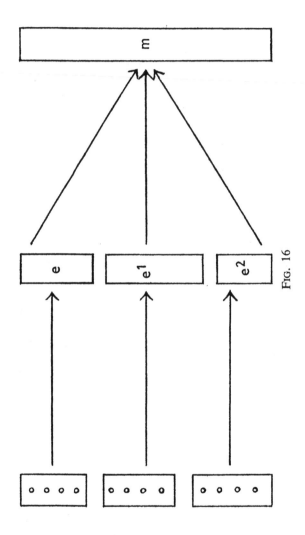

Fig. 16

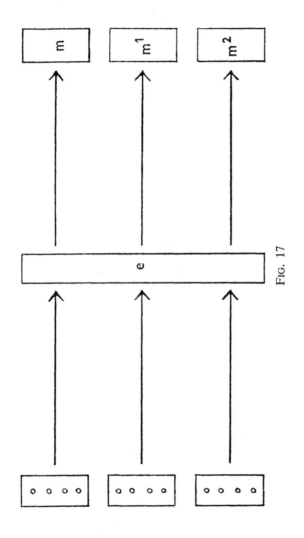

FIG. 17

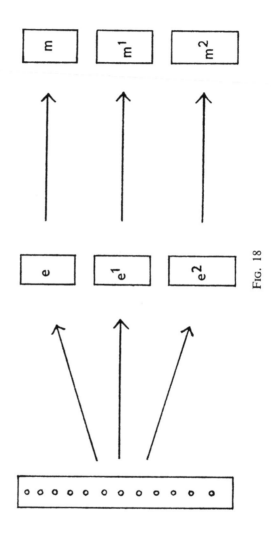

Fig. 18

equipment for various types of materials (Fig. 18). Materials fed to the operatives will require the use of one of three types of equipment. Operatives are accustomed to the use of all equipment. This need to use different equipment may come from the nature of the material; for example, metals of different hardness are sometimes cut on different machines. Or the need may come from differences in the processing various batches have to undergo. For example, timber may be batched according to whether it is to be rough sawn or fully prepared.

Finally, we have the situation where raw materials are grouped for processing by a particular type of equipment, and where operatives specialise using one type of equipment (Fig. 19).

Raw materials may be split into batches that are the right size for each group of men and equipment. Here we have working groups that are more self-contained than under any other form of grouping.

These then are the ways that divisions are made. Now how are they connected again?

Here we need to refer again to what I have already called the link-elements of organisation. You will recall that we picked out three sorts: expression of ideas, exercise of skill and physical change. The last two are link-elements between operative and equipment, and between equipment and material respectively. The first is the link-element between managers and operatives, and it is the one we are concerned with at the moment.

Essentially the link-element between manager and operatives is an authority-link designed to ensure the *co-operation* of operatives. This does not mean that operatives cannot be expected to co-operate without a continuous flow of authoritative directions. A single command may set up a pattern of co-operation that may continue for some time. This activity is carried on through association-links between one operative and another (Fig. 20).

Unless the authority-links are used every so often the activity among association-links will either slowly die out or assume a life of its own divorced from the manager.

The exercise of authority to ensure co-operation we call co-ordination. Co-operation can exist outside organisation, but co-ordination can only exist within organisation where sub-ordination is present. The idea of authority is expressed in what we call orders, commands, or instructions.

D

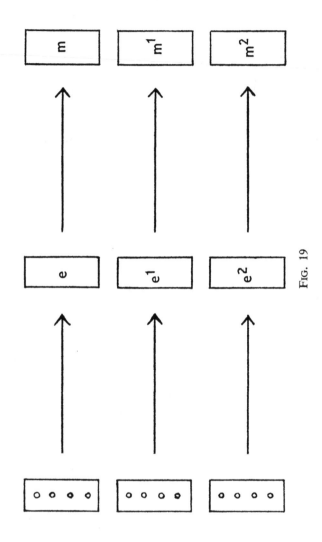

Fig. 19

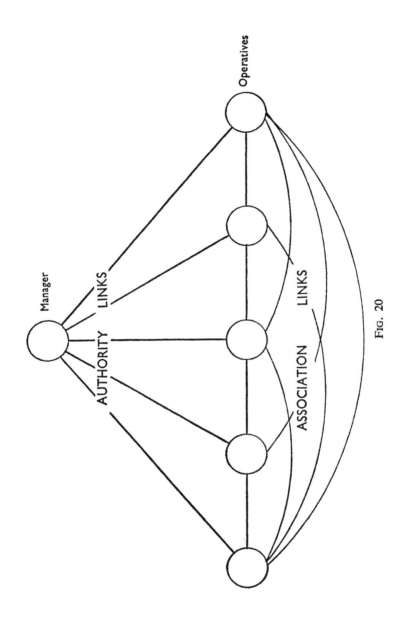

FIG. 20

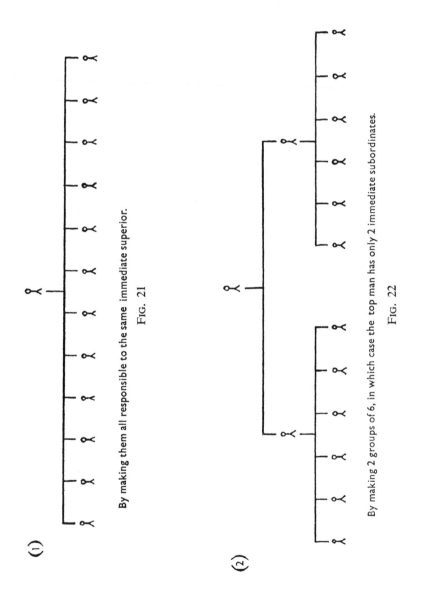

(1)

By making them all responsible to the same immediate superior.

FIG. 21

(2)

By making 2 groups of 6, in which case the top man has only 2 immediate subordinates.

FIG. 22

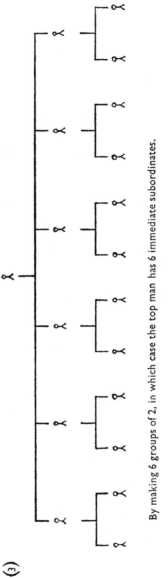

By making 6 groups of 2, in which case the top man has 6 immediate subordinates.

FIG. 23

(3)

The link-elements between managers and operatives are not, however, one-way channels. Expressions of authority flow in one direction, and in the opposite direction information should flow back on the success or failure of subordination and co-ordination.

Some of the possible ways of co-ordinating twelve operatives are illustrated by Figs. 21, 22 and 23.

At this point we must note that if a failure occurs in the authority-link between the top man and a subordinate in (1), theoretically it will eventually result in failures of one-twelfth of the association-links of the whole organisation. A failure in the authority-link betwen the top man and a subordinate in (2) will cause failures in one-half of the organisation. In (3) it would cause failures of one-sixth of the whole organisation.

Number (1) has twelve authority-links that can fail; number (2) has fourteen authority-links that can fail, and number (3) has eighteen authority-links that can fail.

We can now generalise as follows:

(a) If we assume a theoretical rate of failure of authority-links (say one in twenty per working day) any increase in the number of authority-links in an organisation increases the chance of failure of association-links.
(b) The number of authority-links increases one for one with every subordinate added to the organisation.
(c) The addition of intermediaries, between a man and his subordinates, may reduce the *risk* of his individually failing to exercise authority, but it increases the *consequences* of individual failure.

And now, finally, we must look at the major kinds of business effort that engage the men who have to be co-ordinated. There is not a single list that will apply to every business, but the Figure 24 classification is probably as sound as any in that it takes account of a business not as an isolated phenomenon, but as part of industrial society.

In an earlier chapter I referred briefly to certain needs to take external relations into account in organisation. The above

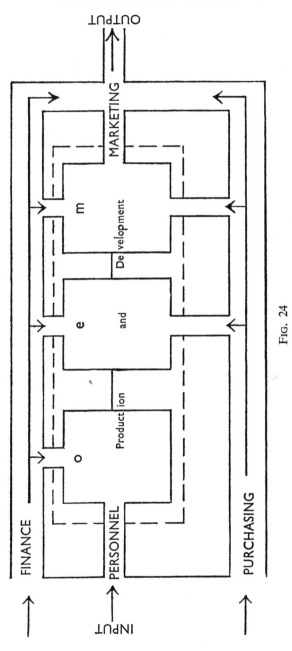

FIG. 24

picture emphasises the need to pay careful attention to the relations that will govern the quality of a business input. Since the three sorts of supplies shown come from such different quarters they exert considerable pressure to group the elements of organisation in a particular way.

CHAPTER X

THE HUMAN ELEMENT
IN ORGANISATION

The practical difficulties of organisation are those of integrating the physical elements; of combining the parts or elements into a whole. The problems may be considered usefully under five heads:

1. that of choosing elements that are the closest fit for the organisation as it stands, and then to alter the elements if necessary to make even closer fits.
2. that of shifting to accommodate elements that cannot be made to fit the organisation as it stands.
3. that of ensuring that each element makes the most valuable contribution it can.
4. that of maintaining elements so that they stay within the organisation, or can be replaced on leaving it.
5. that of establishing a system of feed-backs of the success or otherwise of the measures taken to solve these problems.

In general it is true to say that the task of integrating a number of similar elements is easier than the task of integrating a number of different elements. This is partly because the time needed to become familiar with the common characteristics of similar elements is much less than that needed to become familiar with the individual characteristics of different elements. In general it is also true to say that the task of integrating elements whose behaviour is predictable is easier than the task of integrating elements whose behaviour is unpredictable. This is because in organisation a change in the behaviour of one element calls for an adjustment in the behaviour of other elements, and frequent, unexpected needs to adjust in this way

D*

give rise to strain. One aspect of success in organisation is where each part can rely with certainty on the behaviour of each other part.

The human element in organisation is the most variable and unpredictable. It is possible to buy a number of machines exactly alike, that will remain almost exactly alike, and to obtain the same performance from them. Their capacities can be measured accurately. They will all work on the same fuel. They will all go and stop at the bidding of the master. Although batches of raw materials may not be identical their differences may be stated in precise physical or chemical terms and encompassed by a new machine setting, or process change. An individual does not even behave in the same way from one hour to the next. Human characteristics can never be measured accurately. We are lucky if we can get somewhere near some of the truth; we can be quite certain that we will never get anywhere near all of it.

The trouble is that the psychological outfit of every human being is well hidden away, even from himself. It takes psychiatrists months of delving to begin to discover the truth. And the contents of the so-called subconscious furnish us with the bag of tricks we call our emotions, instincts and so on. We are each of us saddled with what we have got, and without indulging in treatment, must make the best of it.

This means that however clever we think we are in discerning the true nature of people we should always be prepared to face the fact that we have made a big mistake. Organisation must be fashioned on this premise. It must be designed and regulated so that when the human element turns out to be what it was thought not to be, then organisation must react. In many cases organisation must react by expelling the person who does not fit; in other cases it may be able to accommodate the person elsewhere. If organisation is so rigid that it can do nothing to correct mistakes in choosing people to work in it, then it is on the road to self-destruction. This is why a policy of complete security of employment is impracticable.

This is not to say that it is useless trying to take care in choosing people for an organisation. A careful, methodical approach to the task can reduce mistakes; all I am saying is that it can never eliminate them.

In order to be methodical in our approach to the problems

associated with human beings in organisation we should attempt some sort of classification of human characteristics. As C. S. Lewis[1] says 'we cannot hold together huge masses of particulars without putting them into some kind of structure . . . all divisions will falsify our material to some extent; the best one can hope is to choose those which will falsify it least'. The table given on page 108 is one kind of structure, and I hope it does not falsify the picture of a human being too much.

Many words are used to indicate mental and physical powers, for example: capacities, abilities, aptitudes and talents. The word 'capacities' is useful in that it gives an idea of extent and volume, but I prefer the use of the word 'endowments' to indicate all those free gifts of nature that are our intelligence, good health and so on.

A great amount of attention has been paid to the study of mental endowments. Psychologists have sorted them into four main groups; intelligence (sometimes called general intelligence or G), verbal facility, number facility and mechanical aptitude. Despite the great amount that has been written about it, general intelligence is difficult to isolate and to define. If we can gain some idea of what is intelligence from the tasks set in standardised and validated intelligence tests constructed by psychologists, we may have to resort to descriptions like quick-wittedness, ability to associate ideas, ability to discern patterns and develop logical sequences and argument, and so on. None of these descriptions are themselves very precise, but all together they give a fair idea of what intelligence is. People with high intelligence get a quick mental grasp of situations. People with low intelligence fail to take account of parts of a situation or do not recognise the significance of what they perceive.

Verbal facility is the ease with which one uses words in a precise manner, and number facility is the ease with which one manipulates and detects relationships of numbers. Both these facilities are undoubtedly influenced by general intelligence, and in measuring them there is no known way of eliminating G. Mechanical aptitude is the ability to perform physical tasks and understand the consequences of movement. Once again it contains the irreducible element of G, but distinguishes skill in comprehending and reacting to ideas of efficiency in movement.

[1] *De Descriptione Temporum*, 1954.

			CHARACTERISTICS OF THE HUMAN ELEMENT OF ORGANISATION	
ENDOWMENTS	The individual's physical and mental outfit.	Inherited gifts, that must be developed and maintained by education.	Physique	Including general 'build' and state of health.
	The personal raw materials he may or may not be disposed to use for the right purpose.		General Intelligence	Ability to associate ideas, discern patterns, develop logical sequences, argument, etc.
	Innate characteristics developed to some extent by environment.		Ability to use words	Using words in a precise manner.
	Mediocre endowments may be well developed: exceptional endowments may be neglected.		Ability to use numbers	Ease in manipulating and detecting relationship of numbers.
			Ability to use mechanical equipment	Ability to perform physical tasks and understand consequences of movement.
DISPOSITION	The purposes for which an individual chooses to use his endowments.	Determined by the individual, assisted by education.	Strength of purpose	willpower, initiative, energy, endurance.
			Direction of purpose	judgement, sense of values, morals.
SKILL	The degree to which purpose is achieved in the use of endowments.	Acquired by experience and training	Skill in making precise movement in the right direction, in the right place, and at the right time.	
KNOWLEDGE	Awareness of the circumstances under which skill is exercised.	Acquired by experience, and education.	Fundamental	Essential preliminary to acquisition of skill.
			Associative	Enabling a worker to see his skill in perspective.
			Developmental	Opening up opportunities for wider responsibility.

FIG. 25

Our endowments set a limit to what we can do. But they do not determine our conduct. Unless we are mentally or physically sick our endowments give us plenty of scope for exercising that all-important power of choice: choice to go this way or that way, to help this person or that person, to do this job or that job, to work or not to work, and a hundred and one other vital decisions. The way people choose to act has at various times been indicated by the words inclination, interests, preferences, temperament, attitudes and disposition. Of these I prefer the term disposition.

Not so much experimental work has been done in the field of dispositions, and this is not surprising as there is very little here that lends itself to scientific method. A well-known investigation did little more than prove that the disposition of workers is not entirely controlled by working conditions. But then we have always suspected that the goodwill of men came from something beyond their immediate surroundings; and military services have always appreciated the importance of the thing they call morale.

The sort of dispositions that are needed in business, like initiative, energy, endurance, concentration and keeping one's word are different from the dispositions needed for success in many other walks of life. It is certainly wrong to think that people in business cannot afford to be as moral as other men, or that there is no room for feelings in business. Evilly disposed men can do just as much damage in business as they can do elsewhere.

It is widely acknowledged that skilful management can bring out the best in men and bad management will bring out the worst. This is another way of saying that managers can influence the dispositions of workpeople. And this is profoundly true. Quite simply, for example, the will to work can be destroyed in a number of ways. Failure to recognise good work, failure to penalise bad work—carelessness, or over-indulgence are all pitfalls in man management. If business organisation does not supply educative forces, in the shape of firm, just management, humane conditions and good traditions, the human element will disintegrate. Education has at least as important, if not more important, role than training in business.

The primary objective of occupational training is to equip employees with skilled movement. In this context the difference between skilled and unskilled is not like the difference between black and white. Between the completely unskilled movement and the completely skilled movement, if either exist in practice, is a finely graded ascending scale of skill. An employee may need to be taught a particular degree of skilled movement to produce a specifiable object like a wooden chair. Or, less precisely, an employee may be taught a degree of skill that an employer thinks is necessary for a task, where the product is indefinable. It is difficult to know where to stop in inducing skilled movement into, say, an aircraft pilot.

Skilled movement has certain easily recognised characteristics. It is neat movement in that it is neither unnecessary nor unsuccessful. It is strictly economical. It is smooth movement, because all the component parts are co-ordinated and integrated into one whole continuous movement. Skilled movement is habitual in that it requires little thought, and is always approximately the same.

These characteristics are achieved by the gradual elimination of unsuccessful and unnecessary movement at each repetition. Training modifies and speeds up the natural way in which skill is acquired. The natural development of skilled movement is governed by the tendency for actions that bring pleasure to the performer to be repeated, and for actions that bring pain to be dropped, and the fact that success brings pleasure and failure is displeasing. For example, when a child learns to walk it has among other things to acquire the skill of steering itself through narrow gaps among furniture. In its early trials a moment's inattention may result in a hard knock as the child collides with a piece of furniture. It soons learns to be more careful and look where it is going, and even to give a wide berth to sharp corners and harsh surfaces. Soon it will move round a room unerringly and confidently. It does not have to be shown how to do it. Successes and failures recognised simply as pleasure and pain are natural checks.

It is fashionable at present to argue that the same principle should be applied to our approach to the acquisition of occupational skills. Why do we not do more to encourage the development of occupational skills by the permissive method of allowing workpeople to adjust to their objectives? Why do we resort so frequently to the artificial restraints of training and close supervision? It is said that employees should be 'objective-orientated', and even that management will be improved if it is management by objectives.

It is quite true that an employee can learn his job under the control of natural tendencies. Most men will be happy if they find that the work they have done is successful, and unhappy if they find it is not successful. They will tend to repeat the successful act as much at work as elsewhere. The trouble is that a worker all too often has no reliable indication as to what is success. A young child's skill in avoiding obstacles when it walks results from the obvious nature of failure, immediately recognisable from the pain of colliding. Unfortunately failure at work is not always so obvious. That is why working skill is not so simply acquired as walking skill. What we have to remember is that in the absence of clear guides as to what is success and what is failure, a successful act will be one that the worker *thinks is successful*. This is at the root of many bad habits and much lack of skill, and this fact is of great significance to management. For example, let us assume that John Jones is employed to drive a goods van from town A to town B, unload the goods and return for another load. The standard of driving expected of him is indicated by no more than a simple statement that he is expected to do at least three trips a day. In the face of appalling traffic conditions between A and B Jones develops a remarkable skill in doing his three trips with very comfortable margins at each end. But the maintenance bills for the goods van have doubled. Jones has taken great pleasure in every minute he has cut in journey times because he set his own standard of success as minimum time en route. The facts, that the firm gains nothing from the increased time available for loading and unloading, and that the wear and tear on the vehicle is greater, escape him.

Training should begin at this very point. It should ensure that natural tendencies operate to the advantage of a business by spelling out the signs of success and failure.

From then on training adds to the natural process by demonstration and explanation. By demonstrating a movement and asking someone to imitate it we have narrowed the interpretation of success. Complete success is simply a faithful imitation. The task is then easily defined as that of eliminating all but what is perfect imitation. Explanation should also have the clear aim of eliminating unsuccessful and unnecessary action.

Skill is in the actual *use* of equipment. Knowledge is *about* equipment and its use. There is knowledge that is required as an essential preliminary to the acquisition of skill. It is the amount of theory that is necessary to reduce the probability of practical error and particularly serious error. There is also knowledge that is not strictly necessary for the immediate skill. It is knowledge that enables a worker to see his own skill in perspective, and to become acquainted with associated skills. The resulting increase in breadth of vision should open up opportunities for posts of wider responsibility and, at the same time, improve an employee's will to work.

The classification of human characteristics into endowments, dispositions, skill and knowledge is useful when it comes to considering how people should be dealt with in business. Since endowments set the ceiling to individual endeavour, if there is any doubt about whether they will match up to the needs of the organisation, the position must be made as clear as possible before recruitment. In certain circumstances an individual who is too well endowed for a job may be just as troublesome as one who is under-endowed. There should, therefore, be some form of recruitment procedure within the organisation.

Knowledge and skill very rarely match exactly the needs of organisation when an individual joins an organisation. Organisation must take account of the need for an individual to be trained to meet its requirements, or for him to gain experience before he is fully effective. Organisation must take account of the educational (in its broadest sense) need to maintain proper dispositions in its workpeople.

Sometimes it is necessary to change an organisation to accommodate the human element. It may, for example, prove impossible to recruit enough people of the right calibre for a particular form of organisation, and it has to be changed to accommodate people of poorer endowments and skill. Or it may be found that workpeople in general cannot stand the strain of a particular manner of working, and a change has to be made. Accommodating the human element in organisation means among other things providing suitable working conditions. This includes lighting, heating and ventilation, and equipment properly designed for use by human beings.

There is more likelihood of wasting human beings than of wasting equipment or raw materials. Because human beings are much more flexible they can go some way towards doing things they are not really suited for. It is all too easy for us to condemn a man to go on doing something he is not really suited for because we have judged his whole characteristics on something he should never have been doing. Moreover it is much less easy to detect poor performance in a human being. It is very obvious if a machine is idle. It is not so obvious if a human being is idle. It is obvious if a machine is just ticking over. Many human beings go right through life just ticking over without realising it themselves. Business organisations, and particularly big ones, can become comfortable refuges for people who are ill-inclined to exert themselves. But in a sound organisation managers will always be paying great attention to the problems of getting the best out of their operatives.

The task of 'maintaining' the human element in organisation involves all the issues concerned with rates of pay, sick pay, holidays, career prospects, retirement age, pensions and so on. Decisions in these fields are of far-reaching importance to organisation. Some policies give rise to frequent changes of personnel: others to a very stable labour force. Some make for mobility within an organisation: others reinforce the rigidity that is already encouraged by a number of other organisational factors.

The last of the five heads I gave at the beginning of this chapter was that of establishing a system of feed-backs on the success or otherwise of managerial control over the human element in organisation. What I am going to say next may sound exaggerated, but it is not. Once a manager has set up an organisation one of the most difficult tasks he has is to keep track of what happens within the organisation from then on. In the previous chapter I referred to the tendency for organisations to maintain and even develop a life of their own cut off from the authority of the manager. There I emphasised the *ability* of an organisation to *survive* for a time without being sustained by a continuous flow of authoritative directions. Here I want to emphasise that human beings in organisation, seemingly aware of the need to live on their own humps for short times, develop closed-circuit information systems. I say 'closed-circuit' systems because they exclude the manager, and information circulates spontaneously and in no particular direction. So that an intuitive device for surviving without authority becomes in fact, if it is carried too far, a considerable impediment to the expression of authority. Starved of essential information on which to make correct decisions a manager will inevitably lose control. This may not be immediately disastrous to the business. But it will be disastrous to the manager's authority.

The phrase 'rules and regulations' is very commonly used in industry. More often than not it is used to lump together all those hated prescriptions devised by the employer for the discomfort of the employee! Very seldom is any distinction made between 'rules' and 'regulations'. But probably when the phrase was first used the two words were meant to refer to different things.

Rules are commands, orders or instructions that are issued to compel or prevent certain actions. Rules tell us that we must or must not do something. Regulations are instructions that say certain actions must be carried out in prescribed ways. Rules are more preremptory and bolder in outline than regulations. Rules are made to enforce or restrain, to counteract normal desires. Regulations seek to regularise conduct that normally occurs, but in a variety of ways. Thus 'no smoking' is a rule, but 'smokers must occupy the rear seats and carefully extinguish their butts' is a regulation. The distinction is quite useful to the manager in industry as he may well find that he gets different reactions from his workpeople to the two kinds of orders. Sometimes, for example, employees may resent regulations far more than rules. It is not uncommon to hear a worker say that he does not mind being told what to do, but does not want anyone telling him how to do it.

Rules and regulations are 'standing' orders in that they remain in being until the time fixed for their expiry, or until they are countermanded by someone with authority to do so. For a standing order to be successful it must clearly indicate the circumstances in which it is to apply. 'Never smoke', or 'always keep to the path', or 'lock the door at 10 p.m.' are clear statements of circumstances. But 'pull the cord in case of emergency' leaves room for mistake if what is meant by emergency is not clearly understood. If emergency regulations are to apply when anything unforeseen occurs, then this must be spelt out clearly.

Rules and regulations are important tools for a manager to use in his task of organising. They avoid the need for someone to watch continuously and to repeat an order every time the same circumstance arises. Their purpose may be:

(i) to enable members of an organisation to foresee the reaction of their fellows to certain circumstances,

(ii) to ensure that all members of an organisation are treated alike in order to avoid unfairness,

(iii) to ensure that an action is performed in the best of a number of alternative ways,

(iv) to prevent danger or damage to life or property.

There are, however, many points to watch in framing rules and regulations for an organisation. If they are too numerous they stifle initiative, and cause irritation by appearing to be petty. If orders that have clearly outlived their usefulness, and are thus ignored, are allowed to stand they may encourage a careless attitude to useful instructions. Very complicated instructions may bring about the downfall of straightforward workers and ensure the promotion of those with tortuous minds. There should be no doubt who is authorised to issue or withdraw a standing order. It is generally advisable to make the same person responsible for both promulgation and abrogation. If an instruction is not going to reach everyone simultaneously then it should say when it is to come into effect and make sure that the last recipient is able to act on it at the same time as everyone else.

It is no part of the job of a manager to punish a worker in the way that the State punishes a wrongdoer. A manager who exacts a penalty as a deterrent or even as a reforming influence is stepping outside his rightful role. The basic idea that must underly his disciplinary measures is that both employer and employee have freely entered into a contractual relationship that imposes mutual obligations. The remedy of the employer faced with an employee who does not fulfil his obligations is essentially a negative one of refusing to be held to his own obligations. If an employee breaks a regulation he breaks a contract. He has altered the terms of a bargain and must be made aware that the employer is thus free to alter his side of it. In an extreme case an employer may regard the contract as completely void, and that he is no longer willing to continue to employ a man. It is a pity that this is referred to as the 'dismissal' of a man, inferring a more positive act than what it is in essence.

Employees have a semantic advantage in talking about with-drawal of labour. Why do not employers talk of withdrawal of employment? It would help get matters in perspective. Short of this extreme attitude an employer may adjust his side of the bargain by refusing to employ a man for a limited period. This is called suspension. Or he may say that because of the breach of contract he will regard the employee as less worthy of promotion. This is sometimes called loss of seniority. The mild-est form of action is perhaps a reprimand, where an employer does no more than point out and place on record the employee's breach of contract.

Where an employee's breach of regulations endangers the general public, governments usually make provision for some means of punishing the offender. For example, in the transport industry some employees are liable to prosecution as well as to the remedies of employers. In some business organisations there are procedures to enable an employee to appeal against what he regards as an unjust decision of his employer. In most western countries there are State laws to protect an employee from wrongful dismissal, and in some there are special labour courts to deal with infringements of the contractual rights of both parties.

SECTION II—INDUSTRIAL RELATIONS

INTRODUCTION

The relations between management and operatives have been extensively formalised in what are now usually called 'industrial' relations. These formal relations are centred on issues concerned with the essential 'act of exchange' that is involved in working for a business. The employee exchanges a certain amount of work for a certain amount of money. The exchange may be carefully regulated in quality of work and working conditions, but essentially it is the exchange of work for money.

Industrial relations are based on economic considerations. They are materialist. For this reason many people have taken great pains to emphasise that they are not the whole story of the relations between management and operatives.

There is a danger that people will think that formal industrial relations are the only relations that matter. They may then neglect the day-to-day, on-the-job working relationships of managers and operatives that involve considerations other than the purely economic, for example, leadership and morale. Industrial relations, it is true, do not include on-the-job, working relations. They are off-the-job 'talking' relations.

Industrial relations are formalised in this sense. They are channelled through representatives; they are not direct relations between the individual manager and the individual operative. Each has his mouthpiece—mouthpieces inside the business and outside the business. Spokesmen appear in all but the smallest businesses, and outside the press, political parties, trade unions and employers' associations are all aligned on one side or the other. They are relations conducted within meetings, pre-arranged, minuted and run to a set of rules. Discussion outside of these formal meetings is often frowned upon.

Some thinkers were so worried that this sort of relationship should be considered the heart of the matter that they classified all the other important issues in the working situation as *human* relations. It was as if they considered *industrial* relations were inhuman, and wished to draw attention to the fact.

But if this is what they thought, they were wrong. Industrial relations are only too human. That is the trouble with them. They formalise, and amplify, all the human attributes of greed, pride, envy, jealousy, and so on.

The individual decency of the people in the working situation is all too often overshadowed by ill-intentioned spokesmen who multiply grievances and encourage bitterness. Industrial relations are seldom good. This is one of the facts of modern business life.

CHAPTER XI

INDUSTRIAL RELATIONS

Employers and employees are not the only parties who suffer from badly balanced wage settlements. If an employer is pressed to pay too much he may become bankrupt. The disintegration of resources that generally follows bankruptcy is a wasteful process that causes loss to the community, as well as to those who were engaged in the business. On the other hand employees who are pressed to accept wages that are too low to provide a decent standard of living tend to become politically and socially disruptive. Depressed living standards give rise to social unrest more readily than does political oppression.

But the trouble begins with the initial clash of interests of employer and employee. Theirs is the hand-to-hand struggle of leading protagonists. They are equipped for the struggle with crudely fashioned concepts of economic probabilities and with the crudely fashioned weapons of strike and lock-out. Behind them on either side range the more sophisticated forces of government, church and national press. And running true to form, the supporting troops bring confusion and dismay to those in the front line by bad timing and bad placing of effort through misunderstanding the position of those they set out to assist.

The over-riding economic interests of the two main parties are on the one hand the standard-of-living that the employee insists on and on the other hand the return that the employer insists upon. These two positions are indicated by an employee saying 'I cannot afford to work for less' and the employer saying 'I cannot afford to pay you more'. The return looked for by the employer is an addition to the revenue of his business that exceeds the amount he will pay in wages. He may sometimes take on another employee who only just earns his keep in order to prevent a competitor from entering his field encouraged by

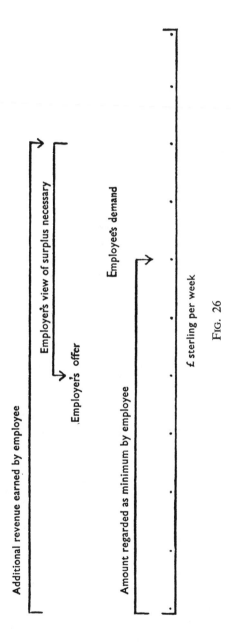

FIG. 26

unsatisfied demand. But generally an employer requires a surplus over wages paid to compensate himself at least for the additional supervision required.

If the employer's maximum does not at least equal the employee's minimum the only possible room for argument is over the employer's surplus, and then only if a reduction of the employer's surplus would bring the two points together.

The diagram opposite illustrates a situation where agreement is not possible unless the employer changes his views on the surplus required.

The employer's view of the surplus that is necessary is influenced by what he thinks he needs to put back into the business, what he needs to reward those who have put capital into the business, and in the end what he considers should be his own standard of living. Different views can be held on all these points and they are all matters that concern employee's representatives at the bargaining table, particularly in those businesses whose accounts are open to public scrutiny.

The above illustration over-simplifies the picture because it shows only one employee and the surplus from his work alone. In a big organisation the overall surplus will present an attractive prize for one group of employees to win not only from the employer, but also from other groups of employees who might feel entitled to lay claim to it.

In many cases, however, there is a gap between what the employee is prepared to accept as minimum and what the employer is prepared to offer as a maximum. This is illustrated by the diagram on page 122.

Neither of these situations will appear in the minds of the two parties as clearly as they have been set out here. Much of the skill in negotiating a settlement lies in concealing one's own position and forcing the other side to reveal the point beyond which there is no yielding. But knowledge of these positions is probably very imperfect at the beginning. Also, of course, the positions indicated in the illustrations are taken up subjectively. They are, as I have said, crudely fashioned concepts of economic probabilities. Even the additional revenue earned by an employee can rarely be assessed precisely.

The gap between the employee's minimum and the employer's maximum is the extent to which both sides can allow consideration to be given to more sophisticated techniques of wage

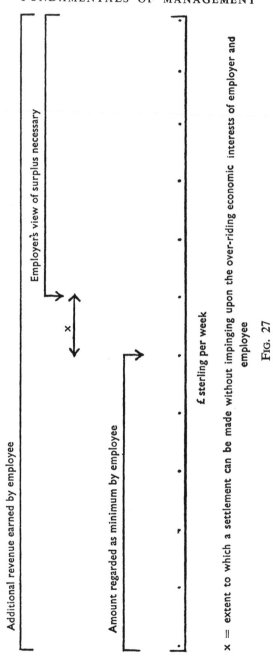

FIG. 27

x = extent to which a settlement can be made without impinging upon the over-riding economic interests of employer and employee

settlement. This is the area in which it is possible to persuade the two to engage objectively in job assessment of individual worth. But what is not always realised is how small relatively is the area in which this is possible. Large organisations usually devote considerable effort to measuring objectively what their employees should be paid. Usually they end up by drawing fine distinctions within a comparatively narrow range of wage rates. Job evaluation is a marginal activity.

This is not to say that because job evaluation is concerned only with the margin left after over-riding interests have asserted themselves it is therefore worthless. Job evaluation can do much to convince employees that employers wish to be fair and at the same time encourage the employer to devote time and thought on what is and what is not fair. But it is still true that when the two points of over-riding interest are close together job evaluation is a trivial occupation.

Nor is it true to say that wage settlement within this margin is very likely to be made by work measurement. The conflict between employer and employee may be carried unabated into this no-man's land and the final position fixed by the bargaining strength of each side. Many trade union officials would much prefer to do away with the employers' measuring devices and leave the issue simply as one of trying to get all one can.

Most employees want to earn what they get. They are much more satisfied if they are convinced that they are doing a job that is valuable to the employer. On the other hand they are dissatisfied if they believe that they are not getting what they earn. This concern for fair wages finds an outlet in arguments over wage differentials and the employer's surplus. The differences in payment that occur on account of differences in degree of skill required for various jobs are usually referred to as wage differentials. Arguments over the employer's surplus usually turn around the amount of money that is distributed as profits.

Most employers will recognise the employee's desire to be paid a wage that is related to the skill and effort put into the job. They may then agree that the wage should be related:

(a) to the quantity of work done, and/or
(b) to the quality of work done, and/or
(c) to the saleable value of the product of work done.

An arrangement that is based on any one of these three, and

excludes the others is not likely to satisfy both employer and employee in the long run.

From the employer's point of view one of the most unsatisfactory approaches to the problem of equating wages and effort is that of paying according to the time spent on the job. Time-rates as they are called are based on the assumption that units of time are rough but reasonable measures of work. The assumption is that a man will do a certain quantity of work of a certain quality and with a certain value in a given number of hours.

From the employee's point of view a time-rate has much more merit. It gives him some idea of what is expected of him for the wage he will be paid. It at least tells him how much time he will have left over in which to recuperate from his labours.

Most good employers admit that piece-rates, whereby an employee is paid according to the number of units of production, for example hundredweights of coal, may place a mental strain on the worker. But they do not agree that time-rates are a fair alternative. Very many men cannot be trusted to do their best if they are paid by the hour. They become time-servers, clock-watchers and work-dodgers at worst, and at best are not likely to work any harder than what will just get them by.

Dissatisfaction with the fairness of time-rates led to the introduction of incentive or bonus schemes. These are schemes that give workers a basic hourly, daily or weekly rate, however small an amount they produce, and add to this guaranteed payment a piece-rate payment for all work that is considered to be above normal. It was thought that no worker need be worried about not being able to work fast enough to earn a decent wage, and yet the fast worker could be rewarded extra. In fact these incentive or bonus schemes have often left the employer as dissatisfied as ever. A trial run, or demonstration of a job, is conducted in which a worker is supposed to reveal the norm, or normal rate of work. But he can and often does cheat. He deliberately works slowly so that the so-called norm that is established is below a normal rate of working. Then the employer finds that he is paying bonuses and incentives week after week merely for an average week's work. He is then in the position of paying a higher time rate, but at least he has achieved a situation in which he spells out clearly what he expects a man to do during his working hours.

In some sorts of work an employer hires a man permanently to do a job for a certain wage, and expects him to do the job no matter how long it takes, within fairly wide limits. The time during which a man is available for work is very much a background consideration.

Although this may appear to be lacking in protection for the worker, he usually finds it an attractive arrangement. It seems to call forth the best in men. It stresses the right thing—the job to be done. But it is an arrangement that can easily be jeopardised by the employer who takes exception when a man turns up one day for only an hour's work, even if he worked for fourteen hours the day before.

There is general agreement that those who 'ply for hire' should be paid for the time they spend waiting for a job. Workers like labourers for the vineyards, ferrymen and film stars are indirectly paid for the time they wait in the market-place until needed by an employer.

Finally, we come to the idea of a wage that reflects the relative bargaining positions of employer and employee. These positions are influenced by how badly the employer is in need of a particular worker, or group of workers, and how badly a worker or group of workers is in need of work with a particular employer. In other words both sides will agree on a figure that seems a natural consequence of how scarce work is, and how scarce workmen are. This may appear to be a simple idea. But it has never worked simply. Economists have praised it as an admirable piece of self-regulating mechanism in the economy. Others have bitterly opposed it as it seems to them to be leaving a matter of vital importance in the hands of blind forces.

The theoretical advantages are easy to understand. The numbers of men seeking jobs can be matched up to the number of jobs there are available by raising and lowering wages. Men will thus be encouraged to go and work where they are most needed and will be discouraged from seeking work where they are little needed. Similarly an employer will be encouraged to take on labour where there is plenty, and discouraged where there is a shortage.

It did not work in the first place because employers were able to make work short, simply by not offering it, whereas individual workmen could not make workers short by not offering to work. The employer could live on his hump; the workers could not.

But now both sides can play the same game. The strike is as powerful, if not more powerful, than the lock-out. Employers are now, and are likely to remain, at a disadvantage. Their abuse of their strength in the past awakened passions that are not likely to disappear for a long time. A show of strength by an employer will always arouse a degree of feeling that is far stronger than the immediate issue merits, as the feeling owes much of its origin to history. Then again those big employers who set the pattern in wage negotiations are usually committed to heavy overheads that eat up at an alarming rate the fat they would have to live on during a close-down. But what is of greatest importance is not the temporary loss of revenue resulting from not producing during a close-down, but the more lasting loss that occurs through customers that go to competitors. In an age that has exalted fierce commercial competition, to stop is almost to die. Employees on the other hand have managed to capture the market in ideas by enshrining the principle of a man's right to withhold his labour. This principle is wholly acceptable if it means that if a man does not like the way he is treated by an employer he should be able to stop working for him and go elsewhere. But it has been extended to mean that if a man agrees to work for an employer one day, presumably satisfied, he may express dissatisfaction a week later by stopping work himself and stopping the employer from replacing him. This extension of the very reasonable idea that a man may withhold his labour presupposes that from the moment an employer engages a man he has, in fact, engaged him on a long-lease that is almost inviolable.

From this situation it appears to me that wages, for some time in the future will move in one direction only, and this is upwards, and that employers will just have to find some way of affording the increases. There is the familiar argument that this will have to be done by raising the productivity of each worker. But the bargainers are not going to wait on increases in productivity, and it is highly unlikely that employers will be able to match productivity step by step with wage increases. So employers will only be able to afford them by robbing Peter to pay Paul. The customer here is Peter, but as most of us are both Peter and Paul the result is not easy to sort out.

Although industrial relations are still dominated by questions of 'take-home' pay a worker's surroundings are becoming more and more important to him. These generally include his immediate vicinity such as workshop, office and vehicle cabin and the more comprehensive environment of factory, office block and vehicle depot.

Reference to a worker's home surroundings has been omitted. We have enough evidence to show that home surroundings do affect an employee's work. We have strong grounds for believing that the influence of the home may in some cases be critical, for example, where considerable alertness is needed to avoid accidents. But we still have much to learn about the interplay of working and home environment and their influence on a worker, and also there is probably little that the employer can do to solve any problem that he unearths.

More attention has been given to surroundings that are man-made than to those that are natural. It is easier to make spectacular changes in buildings and equipment than it is to alter materially the character of field, forest or mine. Not that we should forget the very steady improvements that have been made in primary industries by the introduction of machinery and improved communications.

The influence of working surroundings is not yet sufficiently clearly understood to prevent employers from holding widely differing views. Some assert that surroundings always exercise a profound influence on a worker. Others say that surroundings matter very little. A third view is that surroundings, good or bad, depend for their influence on something else.

The employers' first concern is quite naturally for effects on a worker's productivity. But good employers join sociologists and other students of industrial welfare in concern for the way that surroundings affect the contentment of a worker. Again the good employer is just as concerned as medical officials are about the effect that surroundings have on the health of the worker.

The seven main physical factors that are thought to influence productivity, contentment and health are colour, lighting, noise, orderliness, space, temperature and ventilation. I have listed these alphabetically because there is no order of importance that could be used. These factors are interdependent and, of course, the three properties, productivity, contentment and health react upon one another. For example, a more cheerful colour scheme in a factory may improve lighting; both these may influence the health of workers which in turn reacts upon their productivity. A situation of this sort with so many interacting variables does not lend itself to generalisation. The best that scientists can do to help managers is to explain what is likely to happen to a man if a change is made in one physical factor alone, assuming that one could isolate this factor from the rest.

But of this I am quite certain. In talking of physical surroundings we are talking of something whose importance may be drowned very quickly in the flood of the main purpose of work. Here is a good example of the need for managers to know and even fashion the order of priorities that exist in the minds of workpeople. Our good intentions as managers are always being upset by what are over-riding considerations to the employee. A Churchill, in time of war, can raise the productivity of a nation as he calls for a worsening of their working conditions in a programme of blood, sweat and tears. Yet it is a common experience in industry that passions can run very high over such complaints as chipped cups and draughty rooms. What is the key to this paradox?

It is what the worker regards as essential to the main purpose of his going to work. The British nation saw that it was entirely necessary for them to take Churchill's medicine if they were to succeed in what they set out to do. A worker may well volunteer to work an 80-hour week to get his firm over an emergency, and when the emergency is past begin to grumble about the length of his tea break. Why? It is because he can see the logic of the former, but cannot see the necessity for gulping down a cup of tea in thirty seconds. Coal miners will put up with gruelling conditions underground without a murmur. This is essential. They couldn't earn their money without it. But let the soap be missing when they arrive at their pit-head bath, and there is major trouble. This was avoidable. It was not necessary, but was just employer's carelessness, another example of the general indifference of employers!

Up to now we have talked of direct dealings between employer and employee on questions of wages and conditions of employment. The entry of intermediaries on the scene has not altered the fundamental attitudes of employer and employee, but has often frustrated their aims. These intermediaries are on the one hand the Trade Unions representing numbers of employees, and on the other hand labour relations officers representing the numerous employers in large organisations or Employers' Federations representing big and small firms. So that now it is possible for the simplicity of a duel to develop into the complexity of warring factions. Many managers have experienced a situation in which employees are at loggerheads with their representatives during a struggle with employers who do not see eye to eye with their representatives.

Trade unions officials are professional bargainers. They acquire considerable skill from long experience. Employers have had to counter with the appointment of industrial relations experts to face the union representatives on equal terms. Trade union officials usually study very carefully the business organisations they deal with. The individual official may even have the backing of some form of research organisation at Union Headquarters. It is important for the employer to make similar efforts to study the organisation of each Trade Union he deals with, to know the officials he deals with, and the limits of their powers.

For there is no typical Trade Union. Unions are as different as individuals. They do not only differ in the power that derives from size, but also in the way that power is distributed throughout the parts of the union. They may include in their ranks every single one of a particular sort of worker, so that no one may engage in that occupation without being a member of the union. Or they may have enrolled no more than a few per cent of the total. There is no typical Trade Union official as we are led to believe by films and novels. They vary greatly in intelligence, energy and ideals. Some are weak; some are strong; some are capable of seeing an employer's point of view; some are not. Preconceived ideas based on the generalisation of fiction writers and popular press will not help a manager. He must be prepared to find out for himself, or acquire his knowledge from an expert.

Trade Unions are not organisations whose parts are invariably dedicated to the same purpose, say for example, bettering the lot of their members. Within a Trade Union there may be found four sets of people who as groups think differently. There are the paid officials for whom the Trade Union is the means of earning a living and even a means of exercising political power, or of paying off some old scores against employers. Among them

E

are some selfless men. Some paid officials may do things that are unpopular among the union members, with no fear of losing their jobs, because they are permanent officials who can only be removed for gross misconduct. Others must avoid unpopular moves if they do not want to risk losing their jobs at elections that may take place every two or three years. Then there are the unpaid officials, members of an executive council, branch committee members and so on whose power usually varies inversely with that of the paid officials. In some unions of highly paid employees the most senior paid official, even though he is a permanent official, may be no more than a mouthpiece of the executive council. In other unions the unpaid officials meekly follow the 'advice' given to them by the paid official.

Then there are the active rank and file of unions. These are the people who attend meetings and use their votes. In some unions they vote as guided by their own consciences, in others members' votes are always cast in a way that has been pre-determined at a political party meeting. The last group is that of the inactive rank-and-file who pay their union dues and do not wish to be troubled further. There is little to be said about this group except that they represent a latent force that may assume power in times of crisis.

The most notable skill developed by the experienced trade-unionist is that of probing the economic weaknesses of employers. There are, of course, the obvious occasions for strike threats when stocks are low or order books are full. But there are less obvious occasions where a short strike can do a dis-proportionate amount of damage to employers. In those industries where there are wide seasonal fluctuations in the demand and the product is perishable an employer can be ruined for a year by a few days' strike. In industries subject to varying pressures of competition shrewd timing may make a strike threat more effective.

The relationship between trade unionist and employer or employer's representative tends to be regulated by the fact that the trade unionist will be rejected by those he represents as soon as it is rumoured that he is 'becoming a boss's man'. This is particularly true of the unpaid official who as soon as he learns to look at both sides of the question is removed from office and replaced by someone whose mind is made up and is less likely to be influenced by the facts.

CHAPTER XII

THE NATURE AND TASK
OF GENERAL MANAGEMENT

The term 'general management' is widely used in business. Writers often express concern over the small number of men and women who are suitable for the work. Business men talk of it as if it were a particularly difficult branch of management.

The label 'general' is used to distinguish one sort of management from another. The other sort may be referred to as special management, although in another context it may be called functional management. General management is part of the overall task of management and special management is the other part.

The mental distinctions made in business are not always helpful. Their labels often indicate differences that are more apparent than real. They are the result of muddled thinking in the first place, and it takes some hard rethinking to get back to the fundamental truths. Besides this, almost any analysis of an organisation will help your understanding of it in one direction and hinder your understanding in other directions. The analysis of management into general and special is no exception to this rule.

Having given this warning I can now more safely say that the distinction between general and special management is a useful one.

The chart on page 132 is intended to highlight certain differences that justify the classification.

In some business organisations a man who is called a general manager is not the sort of general manager I have here described. The term is sometimes used more as an indication of rank than anything else. For example, a number of sales managers may report to a more senior manager who is called the

General Sales Manager. Although the various sales managers cover different areas or different products, I would not regard their functions as being sufficiently different to be considered as more than one kind of business effort. So the task of the

Basis for Classification	General Management	Special Management
1. Breadth of responsibility.	Responsible for two or more kinds[1] of variable[2] business effort.	Responsible for only one kind of variable business effort.
2. Demands of the task.	To optimise the result of two or more kinds of variable effort.	To maximise the result of one kind of variable effort.
3. Attitude required of the manager.	To judge an optimum position from the evidence of specialist claims.	To advocate a maximised result from a specialist effort.

[1] We cannot be sure that any list of kinds of business effort is the best for any particular business. The most widely recognised kinds of effort are finance, purchasing, production, marketing, administering to personnel, and development. They are activities fairly easy to identify in most businesses, and that give rise to conflicting claims on the total resources of the business. But these two qualifications may require the list to be extended for some forms of business.

[2] In the sense that the effort may be reduced or increased.

FIG. 28

General Sales Manager is not the same as that of general management defined above.

In practice we find that general management is exercised in one of three positions:

1.

General Manager and Head of the Business					
Special Managers					
Finance Manager	Purchasing Manager	Production Manager	Marketing Manager	Personnel Manager	Development Manager

FIG. 29

2.

Head of the Business					
General Manager					
Special Managers					
Finance Manager	Purchasing Manager	Production Manager	Marketing Manager	Personnel Manager	Development Manager

FIG. 30

or similarly

Head of the Business											
General Manager—Division A						General Manager—Division B					
Special Managers						Special Managers					
F	P	P	M	P	D	F	P	P	M	P	D

FIG. 31

3.

General Manager and Head of the Business											
Heads of Special Aspects of the Business											
General Manager—Division A						General Manager—Division B					
Special Managers						Special Managers					
F	P	P	M	P	D	F	P	P	M	P	D

FIG. 32

For simplicity these diagrams show general management covering all the six common kinds of business effort. Very often, however, a general manager will cover fewer. For example, purchasing, production and development might be put together in this way:

General Manager and Head of the Business					
Special Managers			General Manager		
Finance	Marketing	Personnel	Special Managers		
			Production	Purchasing	Development

FIG. 33

The analysis made in Figure 28 gave us some idea of the internal relations of general management expressed in certain concepts. If we now restate these in terms of personal relations we may say that a general manager has to answer to someone for the way he chooses to optimise different kinds of business effort. In an organisation illustrated by Fig. 29 the one man in his role of general manager answers to himself in the role of head of the business. Figs. 30 and 31 illustrate organisations in which the general manager answers to some other person or persons acting as head of the business. Fig. 32 illustrates a situation in which a general manager has to answer to a number of special managers who filter his responsibility to the head of the business.

The head of the business may be an isolated person, as in the case of a business owned by one man, and managed by another, or the head of a business may be someone who is accompanied in all his decisions by colleagues whose influence may vary from the insignificant to the considerable. Such a head is usually called a chairman, and he and his colleagues are collectively the Board. The chairman's colleagues on the Board are usually referred to as directors, but in some large organisations they are called Board Members, and the term 'director' is used as a title for the specialist heads immediately below a managing director. By definition a managing director is a general manager and not a special manager.

This confusion in the use of titles in business organisations makes it essential for anyone wishing to understand a particular organisation to go through the general thought processes of this chapter. Only by establishing in your own mind some familiar and fundamental ideas of organisational roles will you ever be able to get a true picture of individual organisations.

Your task as a student of organisation is to define the basic roles you are likely to come across, and identify them in your mind by the consistent use of labels, and then to measure the titles and roles employed in practice against the yardstick of your own 'theoretical' organisation.

The general manager has to convince the head of the business that what he is doing is the best that can be done with the resources available to him. He rightly expects help from the head of the business. To do his job he needs guidance by encouragement and warnings. Where the head of the business is a Board chairman there are two possible ways of linking the general manager to him. One way is to make the general manager a member of the Board. In this case he is usually called a Managing Director. The other way is to have a general manager not on the Board reporting either through a Director or straight to the Chairman. The first situation enables the general manager to use the influence of the directors on the chairman, but in turn subjects the general manager to pressure from a number of people. The second situation is simpler, less flexible and leaves the general manager wondering what goes on behind his back.

A general manager's relations with special superiors are based upon the authority of the latter to establish standards that the former is required to follow in the exercise of his own authority. This arrangement makes for organisational difficulties. In theory none of the special heads have complete authority over the activities of the general manager; but the partial authority is enough to make it appear that the general manager has a number of bosses.

The general manager's relations with his subordinate special managers are similar from one organisation to another. In all cases the relationship between general manager and special manager is based upon the authority of the former to grant or withhold resources requested by the latter. The dynamics of the relationship depend to a large extent upon the initiative of the special manager because he is a specialist. Targets are passed to special managers by or through general managers, but the crucial test comes in meeting the demands made to achieve the targets.

A general manager has first to examine the claims made by his special managers. From the conclusions that result from his examination he must decide the merit of the claims. Where the total claims arising from the specialists exceed the total resources available to meet them, he has either to establish priorities so that some are met in full and perhaps some not at all, or to scale down each claim so that all are met in part. Another way of looking at this is that where various claims conflict he must resolve the issue in favour of one specialist or another.

There are three main causes of failure in the relationship between general manager and special managers. It may be argued that these causes are ultimately rooted in human nature, but the immediate causes are in the hands of general managers with whom remedies lie.

Firstly, a special manager should not be expected to do his own job and that of the general manager. It is asking too much for him to put forward the strongest arguments in support of his claim, and at the same time weaken them by conceding rival claims. Circumstances compel the specialist to be in a sense narrow-minded. Secondly, a general manager must be a realist in considering the motives of his subordinates. Men in business are just as good, and just as bad, as they are in private or political life. We are all aware from our reading of history of the treachery, pride, lust for power, fanaticism and other follies and corruptions of men. Business men are made of no better stuff. They may have less opportunity to go to extremes. Organisation should be fashioned to constrain them. But we have enough evidence to show that business men can be evil. At least it is necessary to face up to the fact that a special manager's claims are often shaped by a desire for personal gain.

Thirdly, it is no good making a decision to regulate the conduct of special managers and leaving it at that. As soon as a decision is made a specialist is likely to begin 'interpreting'. This means he will regard it in a manner that is most favourable from his point of view. Very few decisions are worded so clearly that they leave room for no doubt, and it is the margin of doubt that provides the specialist with the opportunity to out-manoeuvre his general manager. The specialist who coolly weighs the consequences of ignoring the instruction is by no means a rare creature. And the temptation for him to ignore it is even stronger if he feels secure in the belief that difficulties in understanding his speciality will cloud the issue. A general manager must watch carefully to see whether his rulings are observed, and if necessary have the courage to enforce them.

Further weaknesses may be found among general managers. Some of them spend too much time on the problems of the special manager whose speciality was once theirs. This does not necessarily mean that an ex-engineer general manager will yield more readily to the demands of the engineering manager. More often the opposite is true. The engineering specialist finds it harder to get his arguments accepted, just because the general manager by training is able to provide exceptional counter-argument; whereas the general manager may give another specialist too much freedom because the former does not understand the latter's skill and is afraid to meddle. But the worst weakness and the most appalling on occasions is where a general manager sits back and lets the warring specialists resolve issues by displays of individual strength, not of argument but of bargaining position.

Judges are customarily recruited from the ranks of advocates. It is generally believed that their ability to judge is helped by their first-hand experience of the ways of advocates. I believe that the same advantage is possessed by the general manager recruited from the ranks of specialists. Increasingly, this is becoming the normal avenue for the aspiring general manager. It is up to him to remember from his own experience all the temptations to which the specialist is exposed.

The head of a business should be aware that the greatest strains in his organisation will be experienced at the junctions of general and special management. At these points connections may be weakened so much that whole sections of an organisation may be cut off from the main body.

A connection has to be made between managers who are 'poles apart' in their thinking. They have aims that differ fundamentally. Conflict is inescapable because it is inherent in the relationship of general and specialist. If specialists set out to co-operate and compromise they may cripple the vitality of approach to their own problems. Their co-operation must be enforced rather than expected.

For this reason the connection between general manager and special manager calls for strong authority to be exercised by the former. There has been a lot of talk about permissive and democratic forms of management. If there is a suggestion of

E*

weakness in these forms then there is no place for them at a junction where strife is continual. The King must remain in control of his barons, otherwise he will find himself confronted one day with a business-like equivalent of the Magna Carta, and some time later he will experience a business equivalent of the Wars of the Roses.

Not that struggle in organisation is confined to these junctions. They are points where the conflicts are most pronounced and most critical. But the nature and extent of the struggles are reflected in other parts of the organisation. Organisation is a struggle. It is not something you do and forget about. It is a continual task. It is a task of keeping people in their place, of seeing that they do what they are supposed to do, and of seeing that they do not do those things they are not supposed to do.

CHAPTER XIII

FINANCE MANAGEMENT

Authority over activities associated with financing a sizeable business is normally delegated at some point to a special manager. Exactly where delegation to a specialist begins varies from business to business. But it depends to some extent on which aspects of finance management are delegated by the head of the business.

The main financial activities are:

1. borrowing money for the needs of the whole business,
2. ensuring that lenders' funds are retained by the business and not dissipated,
3. keeping a situation that enables individual lenders to withdraw funds,
4. paying a fair price for the use of lenders' money,
5. ensuring that lenders' money and business revenue is fed to the elements of the organisation in the right proportions and at the right time,
6. seeing that the money that is fed into organisation is not wasted, or used in an unauthorised manner,
7. calculating profit, and in its distribution balancing the claims of the business and lenders of capital,
8. preventing book values of capital from diverging too far from market price,
9. choosing and using good accounting tools,
10. controlling accounting, statistical, and bookkeeping staff.

Authority over one or two of these activities might, for example, be delegated to an accountant in a Secretary's Department. A few more might be added in delegating to a Chief Accountant, and many more if a Financial Controller is appointed to the Board.

Money to furnish the capital of business (which may be broadly identified as cash and the equipment and raw materials elements of organisation) may be borrowed in a number of ways. The general public may be invited to invest; loans may be obtained from banks; credit may be obtained from suppliers. Whichever way it is done there is room for bargaining. Money is a commodity. Just as with any other commodity it can be bought and sold. It has prices, and there are good bargains and bad bargains.

If money is bought at too high a price then it makes the elements of organisation too costly. It is true that this will be only a temporary phase if there is no difficulty in repaying the high price loan and getting a cheaper one. But the temporary effect can still be just as serious as buying a batch of raw materials at the wrong price.

Price differences are not usually great from one place to another at any particular period in time. The market is so keen that big differences get smoothed out quickly. But the price of money can vary considerably from one period of time to another. If a finance manager is aware of an iminent rise in interest rates and knows that his business will need money in the near future he may do well to get the money ahead of the time it is actually needed. For example, let us assume that a manufacturer will need to spend £50,000 on buying additional equipment in a year's time. He can obtain the £50,000 now at 5 per cent, but is confident that in a year's time he will have to pay 6 per cent. At 5 per cent the interest will be £2,500 p.a. At 6 per cent it will be £3,000 p.a. By borrowing now at 5 per cent a year's interest will be 'wasted' unless the money can be re-lent for a year. But in ten years the gain from anticipating the rise in interest rates is substantial (Fig. 34).

To be able to make the best match between the needs of the business and changing rates of interest, two things are necessary. Firstly, the finance manager must have his ear to the ground to get quick and reliable information on prospects in the money market. This may involve employing an economist to forecast national trends. Or it may be achieved by having a Banker on the Board of Directors. Or it may be achieved by relying on a broker or a local bank manager.

At the same time the finance manager is obliged to obtain information on all important policy decisions, as these will

		Interest p.a. at 5 per cent	Interest p.a. at 6 per cent
Year	1	2,500	
	2	2,500	3,000
	3	2,500	3,000
	4	2,500	3,000
	5	2,500	3,000
	6	2,500	3,000
	7	2,500	3,000
	8	2,500	3,000
	9	2,500	3,000
	10	2,500	3,000
		£25,000	£27,000

FIG. 34

undoubtedly affect the flow of money to the business. For this reason special finance management often occurs at the highest level of organisation.

From this it can be seen that the special finance manager has to maintain good relations with people in the money market, and people in the business who make the major spending decisions.

His relations with people in the money market will be profoundly affected by how carefully he looks after the money he has already got. He will not be welcome unless he has managed to retain what was entrusted to him; if he has allowed resources to be dissipated he will not be allowed further resources to dissipate.

The trouble is that what is bought with money usually cannot be resold for as much as was first paid. Secondhand values are generally below new values for a number of reasons. Equipment begins to wear out as soon as it is used. An improved design is just that little bit nearer. So money must be put aside from revenue to make up for the loss. A provision of this sort is called depreciation.

In many businesses there is an ever-attendant risk of equipment suddenly becoming valueless, because new types of equipment have been invented. Then it is quite uneconomic to go on using the old equipment, because it produces an inferior product, or because its running costs are so high in comparison with the new equipment. In this situation the old equipment is referred to as being obsolescent. It may be almost brand-new and in nearly perfect working condition, and yet be obsolescent. The finance manager cannot fully protect lenders against this risk. It is one of the risks of business that is compensated for in payment for the use of money.

Another risk, or uncertainty, is that equipment may become valueless because the bottom drops out of the market for the things it makes. This may happen because of a small change in taste or the arrival of a completely new substitute that makes old products out-of-date. Again, the finance manager can only partly provide for uncertainties of this sort. Part of the risk must be borne by the lender. In order to give a 100 per cent cover it would be necessary to make depreciation 100 per cent in the accounting period!

One of the most important tasks of finance management is to decide what reserves to create from yearly revenue. In this way they will be balancing the short-term interest of investors, or lenders, against their long-term interests. But also they will be balancing the short-term interests of lenders against the long-term interests of employees.

An obligation to shareholders allied to those dealt with above, is the duty to make it as easy as possible for the individual lender to withdraw his money from a business. The root of the problem is this. The assets of a company are in total worth more in a 'going concern' than when they are dispersed. This is why the liquidation of a business is usually such a serious step. The break-up value of a business is often not sufficient to enable it to return all that is due to every lender.

In general the only safe way of changing lenders is to do it in small doses. Lender after lender in turn can withdraw his stakes as long as he is replaced by another. The ability of the business, or the lender, to find someone to take over will depend upon the good name of the business; and it is one of the most vital tasks of finance management to preserve that good name.

Interest, or dividends, the price paid for the loan of money, should take all risks and uncertainties into account. Where a fixed rate of interest is agreed between lender and the business the position is fairly simple. Considerations of risk and un-certainty must be embodied in a once-and-for-all decision that is not likely to vary beyond narrow limits. Lenders of money at fixed interest rates usually secure their loans tightly. But it is no simple matter when it comes to deciding how much to distribute to what is sometimes called 'risk' capital. Here finance management has to decide every year, or even at six-monthly intervals, how much to reward lenders who are risking their money, employees who are staking their personal efforts, and customers who have some claim on the interest of the management. So much for the major obligations that govern the relations between finance management and people in the money market. Now we must turn to relations with other parts of the business organisation. The most important task here is to feed money to the elements of organisation in the right proportions and at the right time.

We say that we expend the money that is fed into organisation. Expend is not the best of words to use because it gives the wrong impression that something is used up, whereas in a good business it should be converted into something more valuable. Invest is a better word; but there it is, everyone uses expend.

Expenditure can be capital expenditure or income expenditure. The former is money that is obtained from borrowers and fed into organisation. The latter is revenue obtained from selling the product, and fed back into organisation (Fig. 35).

A business organisation is partly self-financing, so finance management has to control the supply of income expenditure as well as capital expenditure.

One of the most effective means finance management has of controlling the expenditure of capital and revenue is by means of a process called budgeting.

Budgets are working plans that are expressed as quantitative and qualitative results for estimated expenditure, within a certain period of time. For example, we might budget to use ten ships cabins for 50 trips a year to give 1st class passages at a cost of £100 per trip, charged to passengers at £150 per trip. There are capital budgets and income budgets.

Capital budgets show planned additions to the capital of a business, and the way that the capital will be invested in equipment, or research and development. Income budgets are usually prepared in two halves: a revenue (income) budget, and an expenditure (income) budget. The revenue budget contains the all-important forecast of sales. The expenditure budget

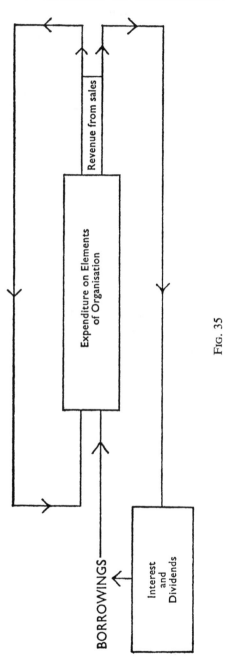

FIG. 35

contains the forecast costs of using operatives, equipment and raw materials to produce and sell the units required by the sales forecast.

Budgets are prepared ahead of the period to which they apply. They must then be studied carefully by the finance manager, who must ensure that his superiors understand and accept all the implications of the plan. Then subordinates will be authorised to work in accordance with the plan. During the working period the finance manager has to furnish continually, information that will enable other managers to compare what they are in fact doing with what they had forecast they would do when submitting their budgets. The same information in compressed form is supplied to top management. So if revenue does not come up to expectation it should be possible to revise plans to limit expenditure accordingly. Information must be supplied promptly to enable the business to act on any conclusion drawn from comparing actual and budgeted revenue and expenditure.

Budgetary control and costing are both aspects of what has now come to be called management accounting. Costing aims fundamentally at establishing the truth about the sectional costs of business in order to discover which sections are not earning their keep. The other main branch of accounting is called financial accounting. Information is obtained from financial accounting too long in arrears to help with the day-to-day control of a business, but it is indispensable to top management in the implementation of their financial policies.

Financial accounting is the tool used by management to turn general ideas into precise and detailed form. It allows the business to estimate the profits that are left after the struggle to balance all the various claims made on the organisation, both from within and from without. It records the calculable safeguards of insurance and maintenance, and the expressions of opinion underlying provisions for depreciation and other reserves.

Nemesis awaits the business that does not record true values. It may either collapse suddenly because it has been milched of its organisational elements, or it will become a prey for the take-over bid, because somebody sees that there is a good profit to be made by taking over some undervalued assets. It is the responsibility of finance management to furnish a business with accounting procedures that are adequate for the task of safeguarding assets.

Accounting records must also provide means of controlling receipts and payments, and at the end of the accounting period to present accurate statements of profit or loss, liabilities and assets.

The operatives in a finance department may be grouped in a number of ways. One group may deal with purchases, and another with sales. One group may deal with initial entries and another with final accounts. Usually budgetary control and costing are carried out by separate groups. But modern accountancy equipment, especially electronic data processing, is imposing entirely new groupings in finance organisation.

Accountants are often said to be difficult people to manage. It is quite true that the long, thorough training of an accountant gives him a mental discipline that he tends to use in his approach to all problems. I think it unjust and organisationally unsound to expect the accountant to present anything but the accountant's point of view. That is what he is there for. If we do not like his answer we should turn to the economist, or better still to the general manager.

CHAPTER XIV

PURCHASING MANAGEMENT

In the theory of organisation expounded in Chapter VI we saw that there were two main ways of doing business: by organisation and by contracting. The finance manager has often some choice in how much work he gets done within organisation, and how much by contracting. He may employ an economist or pay fees for advice from a consultant. He may employ a Cost Accountant or pay fees for one, and so on. A marketing manager may often choose between hiring his own salesmen or selling through agents. A personnel manager may decide to hire fully trained men, or bring in untrained people and do the training himself. A development manager may commission a research institution to do a job for him, or decide to undertake the project himself. These forms of specialised management are not committed to the one way of doing business or the other.

By the very nature of their specialisation, purchasing managers and production managers are committed to contracting and organisation respectively. Their jobs are complementary. For this reason there must be the closest organisation links between them. In some organisations one of them is subordinated to the other to ensure that their activities dovetail completely.

Which one is subordinated to which may depend upon the relative importance of contracting and organisation in the business. In retail stores, for example, where the production process is simply transporting, storing and displaying, the buyer is all-important. In aircraft maintenance where the production process is highly technical and closely scheduled the production manager takes precedence.

But whatever is the organisational position of the purchasing manager it must not be allowed to obscure the essential nature of his job. Basically he buys stuff with just that degree of 'unfinish' that the business wants in order to fully employ its organisation. The mistakes made by a purchasing manager will show up in organisation elements being partly idle, or in their being over-stretched. Having set up an organisation, as an instrument for a certain purpose, it must be continuously fed with material for which it was designed.

The purchase of equipment, especially large pieces of machinery, is important to the economy of the business. But the decision to buy this or that usually turns upon technical considerations, and does not immediately involve the more usual concerns of the purchasing manager over contract price, lead times, regularity of supplies, and so on. Indeed, decisions of this sort are not usually delegated to a special purchasing manager. They are usually retained in the hands of the general manager.

Special purchasing managers are often indirectly concerned with capital equipment, even though they may not be responsible for its initial purchase. The task of buying spares for equipment is often delegated to them. Spares are replacements for worn-out or broken-down parts. A business that buys these spares decides, in fact, that it does not want to repair parts that have become useless but will maintain the equipment by contracting. Any maintenance organisation that relies on stocks of replacement parts is relying heavily on contracting, and the continuity of the production process depends upon the skill of the purchasing manager.

He cannot easily avoid trouble by providing the business with ample stocks. For one reason or another he is usually pressed to keep stocks to a minimum. Nobody likes to see a lot of capital locked up in spares. It is all too apparent that they are not earning any money, and at best can be regarded as a necessary insurance. Inescapably they cost money to store. Interest must be paid on the money spent on their purchase, and rent must be paid for the building in which they are housed, and wages must be paid to the people who guard them and record them. But keeping spares to a minimum in a particular business means that buffer stocks must be kept by the manu-facturer. Somebody must keep stocks if supplies of replacements are not to be governed by the vagaries of production and demand. A business that decides against keeping adequate stocks in its own organisation is really contracting the job to the manufacturer. The more that this is done the more onerous is the task of the purchasing manager, as he has to keep a close watch on his suppliers to see that he does not get let down.

He should exercise his vigilance against the background of an exacting contract. Although he may rely for most of the time on friendly relations that he sets out to cultivate, there will usually come a time when legal, contractual relations are the only real safeguard for a business. Every purchase is in law a contract. Even though there is nothing in writing the law still has plenty to say about the rights and responsibilities of the parties to a contract. Purchasing organisations must either contain within organisation or obtain from outside sound advice on contract law.

The relationships that a purchasing manager will seek to govern by contract will, of course, vary from transaction to transaction, but we can look at a few examples. It is generally necessary to agree some formalities in accepting purchases made. It might be that goods are first taken in for a thorough examination to ensure that they are up to specification, and that they will not be 'accepted' in the legal sense until this is confirmed by advice note to the sender. It is often advisable to establish that 'time is the essence of the contract', and that if goods are not delivered on time, they might as well not be delivered at all. It may be necessary to lay down precisely the way in which goods will be packed. It is always necessary to be quite clear as to exactly what the price quoted includes. Does it include packing, transport, storage charges, and so on?

The purchasing manager may wish to disclaim responsibility for infringement of patent rights; and he may wish to obtain from the seller an undertaking to replace any parts that are defective. He may decide to stipulate how any disputes are to be settled, i.e. by arbitration or by court of law. This tying-up of contracts to safeguard the business requires the purchasing manager to keep a close watch at both ends of the transactions. He must watch suppliers carefully for any signs of possible failure, and he must watch his own business closely to see where changes in production methods should be reflected in his own relations with suppliers.

Besides spares for equipment, as we have already briefly mentioned, the other major responsibility of the purchasing manager is to provide the business with the third physical element of organisation, i.e. raw materials. Much of what has been said about the difficulty of buying spares applies equally to the purchase of raw materials. But there are some aspects of raw material buying that need emphasising.

There are broadly four basic approaches to the job of purchasing raw materials. These are: opportunity, immediate, short-term, and long-term purchasing. Opportunity purchasing is where quantities purchased are related to price and not to short-term needs of the business. The quantities purchased fluctuate widely around say the quantity used up in production each month. This is because the buyer is taking full advantage of every bargain he comes across irrespective of short-term needs, and is refraining from buying bad bargains, irrespective of short-term needs. Of course, in the long run purchases must be related closely to needs of the business, so that this is only a short-term characteristic. The disadvantages of this approach are that there is a risk of materials not being available when wanted, and the opposite danger of incurring costs by over-stocking.

Immediate purchasing is an approach in which minimum quantities are bought on each occasion to meet production needs and no more. No stocks are kept, so that no costs are incurred. The risk is that slight delays in delivery will affect production. Also the costs involved in ordering small quantities are relatively high, and prices may well be higher than for larger single orders.

Short-term purchasing is ordering sufficiently far ahead, say a month or two, to avoid the risk of slight delays affecting production. But the value of raw materials 'consumed' in production is usually fairly close to that of the current market price of the raw material. This may be thought desirable if the market price of the firm's product reflects the current price of raw materials.

Long-term purchasing is an approach in which the price of raw materials is stabilised by contracting for supplies at a certain price for a considerable period, say six months to a year ahead. This is good business in a rising market, but it can be a costly practice in a falling one.

A purchasing manager's organisation should have effective association-links with the finance manager's organisation because, just as the purchasing manager does not want to overstock with spares or raw materials, so the finance manager does not want to overstock with cash. If information is not passed quickly from the purchasing branch to the finance branch, there is a tendency to create buffer stocks of cash to meet unforeseen demands.

In the organisation of a large purchasing branch or department, buyers are often grouped according to the type of raw material they are buying. This enables each buyer to become thoroughly familiar with a particular material and its market, and for his group supervisor to specialise in the production problems peculiar to the one material. Alternatively, buyers may be grouped according to the type of contract governing their purchases. One group may deal with special contracts where individual arrangements are made on price cover, warranties, delivery, packaging and acceptance. Another group might deal with purchases covered by a standard form of contract. Another might deal with purchases that are not covered by any elaborate form of contract, but simply by a purchase order form with no specified conditions printed on it.

Beside buyers there are usually supporting operatives doing clerical duties of a very important nature. Day to day liaison with other departments on stock positions requires meticulous attention and a very accurate recording system.

I certainly have not over-emphasised the role of the purchasing manager. It would need a lot more space to do justice to his specialisation. But I will content myself by saying that it is a branch of management that has not received enough attention.

CHAPTER XV

PRODUCTION MANAGEMENT

Before we go on to consider production management, it will be helpful to pause to see if the forms of specialised management already dealt with are organisationally justified. Why specialise managers on finance? Why have specialist purchasing managers?

We can say right away that there are good reasons for operatives to specialise in these jobs, but by itself this is not a complete answer to these questions.

The job of looking after the finance of a business calls for a distinct set of relationships that are not required in any other aspect of the business. These relationships are with a separate set of people, those in the money market. The relationships are governed by an unusual code of honour, trust, weight of the spoken word and legal formality.

The accounting skills needed by operatives in a finance department are different from skills required in other parts of a business. Accounting skills are acquired only after special and often lengthy training. To a general training there must often be added the skill to use special accounting equipment and the knowledge of individual accounting systems. The equipment, whether it be books, calculating machines or computers, is often considerable.

A finance department has an immediate purpose that is ancillary to the main purpose of the business. People who talk as if there is only one purpose for each business are misleading. Even if they argue that the various purposes are in harmony, they are still misleading. There are various purposes in any business and they are not harmonious. They are in conflict. This is because a business is not self-contained. It has a number of separate external relationships, certain internal relationships, and the interests of the various parties, at least in the short-term, are not the same. There is nothing to be gained by refusing to face up to these facts.

Again, the job of purchasing gives rise to a distinct set of relationships. These relationships are not required in any other aspect of the business. They are with a separate set of people; those in a commodity market. The relationships are governed by particular customs and usage and backed by a very complicated body of common law and statutes. The skills needed for the job are distinct: the judgement to be able to buy at the right time, at the right price, and so on. The equipment is specialised to the task, and the efficiency with which the job is done depends greatly on the use made of the purchasing records system. Again the immediate purpose is ancillary to the main purpose of the business, which is to sell and not to buy.

Specialised management in these activities means this. All operatives doing work that comes under the two heads (finance and purchasing) are subordinated to the same manager who stands in line of authority somewhere between them and general management. The specialised manager has authority to achieve a limited purpose which may or may not accord with the main purpose of the business. The responsibility of the specialised manager is limited to a particular aspect of the business. There is a presumption that the skills required for specialised management are different from those required for general management. This point has already been examined in Chapter XII.

So the organisational justification of these two forms of managerial specialisation is as follows. By specialising a manager is able to acquire thorough knowledge of the work done in his particular branch of business, and thus to advocate his interests against conflicting ones. By specialising a manager in such clearly recognisable functions as finance and purchasing, it is possible for general management to limit clearly his authority and responsibility.

Do the same arguments apply to specialisation in production management? If it is not organisationally justified for these reasons, are there any other reasons that justify it?

First we must ask what 'production' is? The immediate reaction of many people to this question would be to say that the production side of the business is the obvious side. It is the other aspects that are not clear. But this is not so. The reverse is true. It is easy to understand what is meant by financing something, or purchasing something, but it is not easy to understand what is meant by producing something. The real nature of a job in industry is often obscured by referring to it as 'production'.

We will establish first what production is not. It is not, as is often claimed for it, the only valuable side of the business. The people who make this claim will usually be found to believe that they are engaged in 'production' themselves, and to refer to people like accountants and purchasing officers as costly folk who do not earn the business any money. But they are mistaken about the nature of business. As we have seen, very seldom is everything that is achieved by a business achieved by its organisation. It is hard to think of any business that does not do some of its necessary work by contracting. And we have recognised the complementary nature of contracting in the purchase of raw materials. Nor is money from sales the only necessary 'return' for a business. Businesses need the goodwill of creditors, and the community. Nor is the only obligation of a business to deliver the goods. Businesses are obliged to satisfy many people besides their customers. They must produce accounts to satisfy creditors, and a certain standard of working conditions to satisfy operatives. A business would not be allowed to continue if it did not produce these satisfactions, whether by organisation or by contracting. It is silly to regard the work done to satisfy the Inspector of Taxes, and the Factory Inspector as a bit of a luxury.

It is also wrong for the production man to regard himself as being the essential part of the organisation, in the sense that every other activity of the business could be contracted out. If my intention is to make money from the sale of shoe-laces I could do it from my own home without the help of an organisation, by contracting everything from beginning to end. Here thought is easily confused by a wrong statement of the intention of a business. If I talk of my business intention as that of making shoe-laces (which it is not really) then I shall hamper my thinking about the true nature of business.

From considering what production is not, we will now turn to considering what it is. When people talk about production departments, they usually mean manufacturing or assembly

departments. In the workshops and the machine shops it is
easy to see the shape or composition of raw materials being
changed. On the assembly line the process of collecting a number
of small parts and building them into a bigger machine is
comprehensible. But it gives too narrow a view of production.

Production is anything that somebody wants done and is
willing to pay for. What they want done may involve digging
something out of the ground, carrying it from one place to
another, changing its composition, storing it, and so on. It is
all production. But let us note right away that *production is a
matching of what is done with what is wanted and will be paid for*.
Not all that is done is production, otherwise the term over-
production would not make sense. That which is done and is
not wanted, or is wanted but cannot be paid for, is not production but over-production. Under-production is doing less
than people want and will pay for.

Production is only that part of business activity that is wanted
and will be paid for. It is not churning out goods and services
that are not wanted.

The something that is done in production may be classified
broadly into altering people (for example, by drilling their
teeth, or carrying them from one place to another), and altering
things. The something that is done is never a pure act of
creation. It is something that is done to something or someone
(and these have been referred to indiscriminately in this book as
raw materials). If we can locate the object of change we should
be able to locate the act of production, because the act of
production is the change that is made.

In a retail shop goods are altered. They have been removed
from farms and factories to a place that is convenient for the
buyer to go to. They are stored from the time they arrive to the
time that the buyer wants to buy them. In a cricket-bat factory,
goods are altered. Operatives reshape timber, assemble and
fix together differently shaped pieces into a standard pattern.
A restaurateur alters goods. He cooks edible materials, and
places them in convenient positions for those who are to eat
them. He also alters people. He gives what he calls a personal
service in that he tries to make his customers feel welcome,
well looked after, well respected, and so on. A transport
operator alters people. He takes them from a place where they
prefer to be less to a place where they prefer to be more.

Usually when a customer goes to buy something, he is paying for a number of changes probably produced by a number of businesses. One may have clipped the material it is made of from an animal's back, another washed and spun it, and so on.

From the point of view of a business its production is the changes it makes for the benefit of its customers, other than the changes that are directly or indirectly contributed by the activities of financing, purchasing, marketing, development and personnel. The customer must indirectly want these other activities in the sense that he is willing to pay for them. And this is not such an odd way of putting it as you might at first think. For example, there are many people who prefer to buy more expensive products from firms who treat their employees well, than cheaper products from firms with a bad reputation for employing sweated labour. The customer when he buys the product of a business is paying for the total production that has gone into the product. That is to say, he is probably paying for the production of a number of businesses; or putting it another way, he is paying for production achieved by contracting (which is through other business organisations) and production within the organisation of the ultimate producer. It is this last element that is production from the point of view of the business we have in mind.

So production, from the point of view of the individual business, turns out to be a residual activity. It is that part of business activity that is definable only by saying what part of total business activity it is not. This makes two, otherwise puzzling, attitudes understandable. Firstly, how can one firm's marketing become another's production? For example, airlines sell a great number of tickets through travel agents. To the airlines this is part of their marketing arrangements. But to the travel agents the job of selling airline tickets is their 'production': their marketing arrangements are concerned with selling their services to airlines and prospective air passengers. The intention of a travel agent is to sell his services as a go-between, not to sell tickets for this form of travel or that. This squares up with the idea previously expressed that production is thought of as what is done within one's own business organisation. Secondly, how can two sets of people within a large business seriously quarrel over who belongs to the production department? Well, they can in the first place because nobody has labelled any activity as 'production', and lots of people have heard of the impressive word. So, for example, we may hear men working in the printing works claiming that they produce the newspaper, and those in the newsroom claiming that they are the people who really produce what the customer buys a newspaper for. But, of course, the truth is that the customer is paying for a number of things: having news collected, sorted, edited and presented in clear type on reasonable quality paper.

At the root of the problem of so-called production management lies the problem of definition. We talk very glibly about production. But people in business usually do not know what is and what is not 'production'. And if they do know that it is the label given to what is left over after some arbitrary decisions have been made about the labelling of other activities, they are uneasy because they want to see a more logical basis for the use of the term. This becomes all the more apparent when they set out to measure production and begin to realise that their measures are measures of arbitrarily defined activities.

However, all that is not financing, purchasing, marketing, etc., is something: and this something, although it is residual and difficult to define, is regarded as being the main task. What is done in a production department is usually regarded as being done for the customer (forgetting for a moment the factory inspector, the trade unions, the local 'smoke abatement' association, and so on). By now you may well be asking where all this leads us to, as it seems so negative. However, it is only when production management has rid itself of all pretensions that the specialisation begins to appear justifiable.

Very significantly we can say that the production manager has to face problems that are most peculiar to his business, and that it is least possible to generalise about them. Another way of putting it is that his problems are the most business-like. Attempts have been made to generalise by classifying production-management systems, for example, into unique production, mass production and process production. These classifications have certainly been useful for some purposes, and they are well worth studying, although I do not want to deal at length with them here. I refer to them only to illustrate the dangers of generalising about the most businesslike residual activities covered by the production label. Underlying mass production and process production systems are ideas of this sort: that the *physical nature* of the product, be it motor-cars or coal gas, should entirely govern the system of production; that the natural wishes of the customer should be changed to fit in with the *best system of production*. We do not do what is best for the customer, but what is best for 'production'. Henry Ford's remark, 'The customer can have any colour car as long as it is black', was not just a joke. It illustrated a belief. Similarly, if it is best to keep the production of clothes going continuously, then the customers must be made to need them continually by rapidly out-dating the clothes they have on their backs. Or if transport systems are best worked for 24 hours a day, we should persuade people to travel around the clock, however unnatural that may be.

There may be strong, valid arguments for such a belief. But this bending of the customer to production systems can go only so far; we must recognise it for what it is. As I said in Chapter V, if we are more concerned with maintaining a particular form of business organisation than with the customer's needs then we are on the road to a businesslike totalitarianism.

We must be realistic and face up to the fact that what customers want (taking into account shape, size, weight, colour, time, place, and so on) even when it is limited by what they can pay for, will be sufficiently awkward to cause waste in business organisation. But here is the whole art—the prime justification for specialisation in production management. *Production is a matching of what is done with what is wanted and will be paid for.* Business organisations can never be as flexible as the demand for their products, so there must always be either some waste or inadequacy. The job of the production manager is to minimise it.

Much of the inflexibility of business organisation is caused by the inflexibility in the link-elements of organisation: the limits of human skill that determine the use that is made of equipment, and the limited changes that can be made by equipment installed for certain purposes and no other. It is the compelling rigidity of business organisations which leads Drucker to say that it is of major importance in managing a business to know which (ideal) system of production to apply. He talks of the logic of house-building, and how it should be done by stages that will enable work to be stopped for fairly long periods without danger to the construction, but in the interests of organisation. This organisation ideal ignores the impatience of the customer, who always seems to want to move in tomorrow, and the pressure from the finance men who want to see money turned over as quickly as possible. I have seen these systems crumble under these pressures, and the foreman puts all his men on overtime and merges one stage with another. This may be bad production management, but it may be good finance management, and good marketing management. And, on balance, it may be good business management.

CHAPTER XVI

MARKETING MANAGEMENT

The whys and wherefores of marketing have been clouded by a spate of literature. People have seen that the gains to be made from trading result from the interplay of human minds. The extent of gain does not have to depend completely upon the wares, because the price that customers will pay changes with their beliefs. Volumes have been written to show sellers how they can change the beliefs of buyers. Seemingly, the language has become more and more scientific, and less and less understandable. Yet the simple truths that underly dealings in a market are the same as ever.

It is easy to see why so much attention has been paid to marketing. The rewards of success can be great; as great as the marketing man deserves, and greater than the production man deserves. A good production man can enable a business to be prosperous by turning out a sound product: he cannot ensure prosperity, nor can he influence the extent of prosperity in the same way that the marketing man can. If the production man makes a good commodity for £1 it would probably 'sell itself' at 25s, but with the aid of a marketing man it may well fetch 30s.

What does the marketing manager have to think about? How does he make for success in his job?

First, he must use, and, if needs be, choose the right market-place. And I am not using the term market-place figuratively. I do not mean something abstract, but a place where people go to buy and sell. We will assume for the moment that buying is done when goods or services are actually handed over to the buyer. Such a place is better if it is well known. This may sound very obvious to the reader, but it should be said all the same, because one of the main tasks of many marketing managers is to make the market-place, in which they sell, well known to all their prospective customers. How many times have you wondered where you have to go to buy a particular commodity, and how many times have you given up trying just because you could not be bothered to go on looking for the market-place?

The market-place is better if it is easy to get to; and in this day and age 'getting to' it should include by telephone, telegraph and post. This is because the buyer now often agrees to buy in the market-place before he actually completes the act of buying by taking delivery of goods and services. The market-place is better if it is easy to stop at. If it lies in the path of people who are accustomed to hurtle by at high speed, it will need to be very attractive to pull them up. The market-place is better if there are satisfactions, other than those of the one transaction, to be had by stopping there.

The market-place may be a single locality serving a nation, and offering no choice to the marketing manager. For some transactions there is no alternative to the London Stock Exchange. For others, Covent Garden is incomparably better than any other. But groceries are sold in many thousand localities throughout the land, and, looked at in one way, every home in the country is probably a market-place for milk, as it is here that milk is handed over to the customer. Perhaps one of the most critical decisions to be made by the marketing manager is whether to deal in nearby markets or go to remote ones: whether to deal in home markets or in export markets, or in both.

The next big task for the marketing manager is to see that deliveries to the market are right. He has to bear the brunt of complaints when the flow of goods into the market do not equal the flow of goods out of it. He is a go-between and is usually in the position of being able to satisfy neither of his principals, the production department and the customers. On the one hand he may have to point out to production management the facts of life in that the buying habits of customers cannot be altered beyond a certain point. On the other hand he may set about persuading customers that in the long run it is in their own interests to adjust their buying habits to accord more with the pattern of production. Persuading them or deluding them may not be enough. He may have to make it advantageous for them to fit in with the organisation of business by making it cheaper for them to do so.

Where a 'market price' prevails there is normally less room

F

for this sort of manœuvre. Market-price is by definition one that the individual business cannot sell above, because it would attract no buyers at all, and one that the individual business does not normally sell below because it can sell at that price all it produces. Market price can be an efficient, automatic regulator of the flow of goods and services into and out of the market. But individual businesses tend not to like to have their policies regulated by what they regard as the impersonal force of market price. So most businesses try by one means or another to become monopolies. Many managers have an idea that making decisions is a lot easier in a monopoly because all the business forces are under their control. This is not true; but it is what many of them believe. They forget the simple fact that even in a monopoly they can only control one of two things. If they decide to control the quantity produced they must leave it to customers to determine price. If they decide to control the price they must leave it to customers to determine the quantity they buy.

The most usual way of making a business into a monopoly is to persuade customers that the business makes something that is made by no other business. Thus a maker of pounds of butter, that are just the same as all the other pounds of butter made by all other businesses making butter, can become a monopolist by persuading people that their Cowslip Butterpat is like no other pound of butter in the market. It then becomes practicable to control its price or the quantity sold.

The third major task for marketing management is to display the wares for as many as possible to see. If the products are wrapped up, the wrapping should be just as eye-catching as any other wrappings and, if possible, more so. The properties that make them eye-catching must be attractive and not repellent. The background against which the product is displayed should add to its attractiveness and not detract from it. The displays of the wares of other businesses should not be allowed to obscure his own. No wonder there is a clamour in the market-place! But it is difficult to see any alternative.

The device of advertising enables the marketing manager to extend widely his display work. The physical limitations on the display of actual wares are largely removed in the symbolic presentation that we get in advertising. So in a sense goods can be displayed even before they are made, and they can be displayed outside the market-place more and more extensively, until we reach the finality of display on television screens within our own homes.

A rather neglected aspect of the job of marketing is the way cash is collected. Much attention has been given to delivering the goods, but very little to the other half of the transaction— taking the cash. There seems to be something in the make-up of most human beings that makes them very touchy if not down-right embarrassed over paying money. No doubt there is some religious idea at the back of it. As the root of all evil, money is not to be handled with apparent relish. Also there are social attitudes to meanness that makes it difficult for the ordinary man (who is not a professional trader) to closely check cash that is changing hands. To counterbalance these handicaps people have developed very sharp reactions to any sort of careless treatment in the handling of their cash.

Finally, there is the very important aspect of marketing: that of deliveries from the market to the customer. Deliveries may be made on the spot, that is, the customer may go to the market to collect, but this does not make any difference to the principles that apply. From the customer's point of view he will probably be more pleased as deliveries become more frequent, because the time he might possibly have to wait will be reduced. The customer will usually be attracted by the regularity of deliveries as this removes the wonder whether if he does not catch this delivery will he have to wait an abnormally long time for the next? A slight delay may not really matter to him a bit, but if he feels it does, that is what matters to a business.

Sometimes speed of carriage or time taken in transit is important to the customer. Again, gains to the customer may be entirely illusory, but it is what he thinks that is more important to a business. And, in a nutshell, what the customer thinks is very much the concern of the marketing manager.

If a marketing manager fails to do what is expected of him, it is only too clear to everyone else in the business that he has failed. Other special managers may escape attention when they fall short of the mark, but the marketing manager cannot. His work is the fulfilment of the intention of the head of the business. He clearly fulfils it or does not fulfil it. As we saw in an earlier chapter, the intention of a business always consists of the two aspects: producing something, then selling it. Thus, the 'pro-ducing-something' aspect of the intention may be achieved, and then the frustration of intention occurs in the marketing process.

It may well be that a business does not succeed in its intention because the marketing manager has done a sloppy job. But equally his task may be impossible because the intention is unacceptable in the market, or that the intention was frustrated elsewhere in the organisation. The ways that businesses commonly fail were dealt with in Chapter V. Although as I said earlier, the marketing manager has the elbow-room to boost the prosperity of his business, we may still give him too much credit for success, and too much blame for failure. There are times when he can do little or nothing to influence business.

Essentially the role of the marketing manager ensures the continued existence of the organisation of a business. For he transmutes all the goods and services brought into organisation, and all the contributions to the business by contracting, into money that can be used to maintain the physical elements. The marketing process feeds money back into the coffers of finance management.

Looked at in another way the marketing manager completes an organisational circuit in which finance is the current, fed occasionally from loans, and from which profit is periodically extracted. This point is worth making because marketing is often thought of by production people as a remote function at the end of a long line of organisational activities, instead of its being on a circle of a self-generating system.

Since it is the duty of the finance manager to ensure that the proper demands for current are met, it is important that the marketing manager keeps him informed on what supplies he can expect from within the system. In some ways planning is a lot easier if the flow of money from the market is continuous and constant in volume. If the flow of money from the market is irregular it is usually very difficult to phase it to coincide with the needs of organisation.

Relations between marketing management and production management are often difficult. Conflict usually arises because one regards the other as being less important. In some cases the production manager believes that the job of the marketing manager is to sell what he makes. In other cases the marketing manager believes that it is the job of the production manager to make what he knows he can sell. These views may be correctly based on the nature of businesses that require precedence to be given to the demands of either production managers or marketing managers. But, if this is so, it is important that the situation should be clearly understood by both specialists, otherwise the decisions of general management will appear to be biased in favour of the one for no good reason.

The marketing manager's approach to customers is in practice broadly influenced by the type of business. Where the business is engaged in 'tailor-made' production he must obtain orders from customers before production begins. He needs to persuade customers that the business can produce exactly to the customers' requirements. He has to demonstrate clearly that his business has skill and equipment of high quality and flexibility. His salesmen must be sufficiently well qualified technically to be able to understand the customers' problems and to be able to discuss these problems on a more or less equal footing with the customer.

At the same time the sales group must be closely associated with those engaged on production. They must give leads to the production side in the interests of the customer. They should be prepared if necessary to give a day-to-day liaison service between customer and production men.

In a business engaged in the mass production of standardised products in practice the sales force aims to protect the economics of the productive process by persuading customers that it is in their best interests to buy goods of a pattern already planned or produced. The arts of salesmanship are more important and the scientific adjustment to customer's needs of less importance than with tailor-made products. In mass-production businesses it is not so necessary for the sales side to work quite so closely with the production side. The production group will need some lead from the sales group, especially at the production planning stage, and they will need periodical 'feed-backs' from the sales force as checks on decisions, but will not need the same day-to-day liaison as unit-production groups require.

In businesses engaged in continuous production (for example, of fuel oil or chemicals) the marketing manager has to establish an assured market before production is started on a large scale. He usually puts out his major effort at an early, experimental stage. After gaining initial acceptance of the product his main task is to see that demand is regulated in accordance with his firm's capacity to produce. It must be stressed that the inflexibility of continuous production calls for the highest quality marketing management.

The marketing manager's organisational groups are usually based upon the different external relations he has to maintain, and the distinct social and technical skills required in dealing with each. There is usually a separate advertising group. Its members must be well versed in the technicalities of printing and other forms of display. They must be well acquainted with the merits of the great number of advertising agencies working in every big city.

Usually the manager has someone, or group, handling market information, and constantly in touch with market research organisations and other sources of intelligence. Another group may deal with selling directly to the customer: another may deal with sales agents if they are employed by the business.

People on the marketing side of businesses are often difficult to manage. The qualities that make them successful in the market are often the qualities that makes them fail to fit into organisation. The flair, the intuitive reaction, the inspired guesses, the brilliant hunches that are tremendous assets in the market become severe handicaps when it comes to having to co-operate closely with other people in organisation.

CHAPTER XVII

PERSONNEL MANAGEMENT

Personnel management is one of the latest forms of special management. Only in the last two or three decades have business men thought it advisable to provide within their organisations managers to deal with certain aspects of the human element. Probably no other form of special management has given rise to so much frustration for the special manager and so much resentment from his colleagues. But then no other form of special management presents such a threat to the essential authority of other managers, and such a curb to unhealthy liking for power that finds its satisfaction in absolute authority.

Since a personnel manager can be a very disturbing influence in business organisation, we must be very sure that it is worth while having him. We must be sure that he does not do more damage than good. I would put the case for having a special personnel manager as follows.

The behaviour of materials is subject to physical laws. These are scientific laws. They describe what actually happens. They do not say something *ought* to happen, but that it will. There is certainty if all circumstances can be controlled or foreseen. Scientific laws are sure because they do not go beyond stating what is. They are not laws that exist apart from the material itself, but are statements of the unalterable nature of things. They are not laws that can be disobeyed. A certain metal will melt if it is raised to a certain temperature in certain atmospheric conditions. It has no choice. It is predictable if circumstances are predictable.

The behaviour of human beings is influenced by the laws of human nature. These laws are not scientific laws. But, nevertheless, they fashion those widely held views on decent conduct that are fundamentally similar in every community. These laws distinguish right from wrong and cause stirrings of conscience, and a natural antipathy to trickery, selfishness and so on. These laws have been variously referred to as the Natural Law, rules of fair play and morality. Call them what you will, they are very important in determining human conduct, and despite all the apparent changes in religious and political beliefs they still represent standards of behaviour that everyone expects everyone else to know about and adhere to.

They are not scientific laws because they do not describe what is. They state what ought to be and what often is not. Human conduct is often contrary to the rules of fair play. For this reason the laws of human nature cannot be framed in the same way as scientific laws, that is from external observation.

It is, however, no good taking up the attitude that because the rules of fair play are not scientific laws that they do not deserve to be considered by a 'well qualified', highly trained, technical manager. It is true that the laws of human nature do not tell us, in fact, how a man behaves. But there are many things that science does not tell us, and never will be able to tell us, and we do not dismiss it for that reason. Nor is it defensible to argue that the laws of human nature cannot be considered seriously because they cannot be proved by external observation. External observation is not the only road to knowledge. We have a unique means of getting to know about men. We are men. We have the inside story.

What is the significance to managers in business of the fact that most men know how they ought to behave and do not, in fact, behave that way, whereas materials always behave in accordance with their nature? Right away we can say that it follows that man management is more difficult than material management because of the unpredictability of human conduct. But beyond this it is not easy at first to see that a manager is at all concerned with an individual's views on decent behaviour. Is it not a purely private matter? A matter for the individual's own conscience?

Until we remember that these laws are what each employee expects every other employee to know about and obey. Although I do not always keep to the rules of fair play, nevertheless I expect other people to keep to them at least most of the time. Breaches of the rules of fair play cause as much trouble in business as they do in the family, or school, or village. And just as the school or state has to base its rules or laws on the laws of human nature, so businesses are compelled to base their rules and regulations on the same principles. Management is concerned with seeing that the conduct of business does not run counter to the fundamental beliefs of men within that organisation.

Most of the mistakes made in dealing with human beings in business organisations are errors of omission rather than commission. Managers tend to be so preoccupied with 'technical' problems that they just do not get round to spending time on thinking about problems of justice and fair play. Some of the best business men, whose brilliance and drive have brought prosperity to a host of workpeople, make the worst blunders in their handling of their employees. And if they devoted more time to the human element in their organisations the businesses would probably soon begin to suffer, and in the long run this would, of course, affect the very men whose welfare was concerning them.

The stern fact that man shall live by the sweat of his brow means that business, like the show, must go on. It may well be disastrous to suspend business for even a short period in order to attend to the maintenance of a part of its organisation. Repairing, refurnishing, converting or replacing parts of organisation are activities best carried out to one side, out of the path of the main activities of producing and selling. One of the most valuable contributions a personnel manager can make is to 'maintain' the human element in business organisation in such a way that it does not hinder the intention of business.

So he may for example relieve other managers of the time-consuming task of recruitment. Choosing the right people for an organisation is as we have already seen an exceedingly difficult task that requires considerable experience and skill on the part of the manager making the choice. A person who specialises in selecting people for jobs acquires skill from experience, and develops methods and techniques that reduce the possibility of error. So the job can be done with a thoroughness that would not be likely if the man was taking time off from what he regarded as more essential tasks.

Some forms of training and education are best done away from the job. There may be some danger in distracting a production man's attention at a critical moment if he has to think

F*

about training as well as attending to his job. Some forms of training require a quiet unhurried approach that is not possible near a production line. Sometimes the interruptions, that are inevitable in a situation where business needs must come first, do not allow a good job to be made of training. So training may be handed over to someone not in the main stream of business activity. Also, teaching is a skill that all but the very gifted take a long time to acquire. So there are considerable advantages to be gained by specialisation in the task.

Somebody who spends a lot of time thinking about the characteristics of the human element in organisation usually has a point of view that should be considered when it comes to making changes in organisation. Trouble often arises in business organisation because of failures to take into account the limitations of human beings. People can stand just so much physical strain, or noise, or dirt, or nervous strain, and no more. A special personnel manager is often in a position to be able to give much sounder advice than anyone else, on what workpeople can take, without getting restive and sick. Because he spends so much time in considering what is human he is well placed to detect what is inhuman.

And the noblest of men, in pursuit of their pet schemes for the benefit of their businesses in particular and mankind in general, can be inhuman. It is all too easy for someone, who is pre-occupied with the details of a piece of new equipment, or some wonderful new raw material, that will bring satisfaction to a great number of people, to overlook the discomforts it brings to those closest to the innovation. British monarchs once had an official who was regarded as Keeper of the King's Conscience. In a way the modern personnel manager is an industrial equivalent of this official. He stands at the elbow of the general manager and nudges him if someone suggests doing something that goes beyond the bounds of human acceptability.

This particular aspect of the role of a personnel manager is delicate and full of dangers. He can easily lose the sympathy of his colleagues by appearing to press the claims of humanity too far. People who argue cases for processes, equipment and other materials are usually considered to be businesslike. As we have already noted, they can talk with the precision associated with scientific laws. People who press the claims of human nature are often considered to be unbusinesslike because they cannot argue from a scientific standpoint. This may be unfair on the personnel manager who is just as mindful of the demands of the business as anyone else is. On the other hand it is right that general management should remain alert to the possibility of the personnel manager getting too soft. The sweat of a man's brow is a metaphorical way of saying that work necessarily involves a certain amount of physical discomfort, inconvenience, monotony, worry and so on.

All of us have parts of our job we dislike, and moments we hate. The personnel manager cannot support people in their restless pursuit of something they can never achieve, that is complete satisfaction with what they have. One of the laws of human nature is that it possesses a hunger that cannot be satisfied. It does not matter what job, what surroundings, what pay, prospects, or boss, we always feel that something has eluded us, and we are always left with a longing for something that will never come within our grasp. I believe that this is how human beings were meant to live—in a constant state of discontent. If this belief is true, then we should watch carefully to see that business organisation is not blamed for something that is inherent in human nature.

One of the most frequently heard comments in the office of a personnel manager is something like this: 'This is a genuine grievance.' Here we have an indication that someone has thought about a grievance and has sorted out the genuine from the not genuine. The latter he would probably recognise as those caused by man's inherent tendency to be dissatisfied with what he has. The former are grievances that arise from enduring malpractices of organisation. This sifting of the wheat from the chaff takes time, requires patience and calls for experience in handling grievances. The advice of a personnel manager can be invaluable to a busy ambitious business man who may be cut off from much direct dealings with his workpeople, because he has a number of other relationships that absorb his time.

In a big organisation the case for having a special personnel manager becomes even stronger. Unless there is someone keeping an eye on the human element throughout the whole business, individuals are likely to be confined to a part of the organisation. An individual manager likes to keep the good men working for him. There is a need for a third party who can advise that a good man should be moved to another part of the organisation, in the interests of his own career, and in the long run in the interests of the business itself.

The larger the organisation the more dangerous it is to rely upon the memory and opinion of any one man. Some sort of personal records will be necessary. The sources of information contained in these records will be based upon reports obtained from a number of superiors throughout the organisation. The information must be recorded in a concise form and stored in such a way that it is readily accessible to people who have to make the decisions that should be based upon this information. There are some businesses that are very busy collecting facts about the performance of their employees, but these facts are never looked at by managers charged with the task of deciding on the future of employees.

We have already seen that a good business organisation specially provides for someone to keep an eye on the interests of investors in the business. By the investor we meant a person who had entrusted the business with some of his money. The investor deserves to have his money looked after because he made a sacrifice in handing it over to a particular business. There were other things he could have done with it, and his supply of money is limited. Rightly enough it is important to him that he makes the best use of his capital, and does not waste it.

How much more important than money are the endowments, dispositions, skills and knowledge of a human being. And these are what a man or woman invests in a business that he or she goes to work for. While the individual must be prepared to accept some risk that the business will fail to make the best of his characteristics, in the same way that the money investor must be prepared to risk losing his money, at least we might expect a good business to take as much care over the personal investment of its workpeople as over the money stakes of its shareholders.

I have left until last the argument for having a special personnel manager to handle the formal industrial relations dealt with in Chapter XI. This is not because I regard these grounds as being any less important than the foregoing, but because they are already much better understood and accepted. The appointment of an industrial relations officer is business's instinctive reaction to the harassing attentions of trade union

officials. And quite rightly so. Trade unions have only themselves to blame if industrialists have felt it necessary to engage
professional negotiators to match the cunning and persistence
of the men they employ to work on their side of the table.

Whether in the long run anyone gains from these incessant
parleys is not the most important issue. What is vital is that
business managers responsible for the prosperity of their own
organisation, and ultimately that of the community, should not
be drained of healthy constructive effort by the time-consuming
irrelevancies that are part of the almost ritual manœuvres of
the negotiating table.

CHAPTER XVIII

DEVELOPMENT MANAGEMENT

We frequently hear people say things like this: 'This business has gone a long way in ten years' or 'You wouldn't be able to recognise this as the same firm you'd seen ten years ago'. These remarks are reflections of the prevailing fact that businesses do not stand still. They progress or disappear. Over a period of time their development is as significant as the sum-total of their production.

Development means change. Businesses change in two main ways. Firstly, they change the design of their products to accord with changes in demand. Otherwise they would not continue to carry out the intention of selling their products. Secondly, they make changes in organisation in order to fashion cheaper ways of producing, selling, financing, purchasing and so on. The former change aims at increasing revenue more than expenditure, or at least to see that revenue does not decrease in relation to expenditure. The latter change aims at reducing the cost of earning the same amount of revenue, or at least to see that costs do not rise in relation to revenue.

Features of the demand for the product of any business are always in the process of change. By features of demand we mean: origin, location, interval and regularity. All feature changes eventually influence the quantity of the product that customers will buy at some moment in time, at the price at which it is being offered for sale. There will be short-term fluctuations around an average figure, but these fluctuations will in all probability be occurring against the background of a steadily growing or steadily shrinking long-term demand. Change in quantity bought may be a reflection of general increases or decreases in the purchasing power of the community. If so it should not be too difficult to establish this fact by studying the various indices of the state of the national economy.

Other changes in quantity bought occur because of shifts in economic preference. More or less of a particular product is bought because people are buying less or more of some other product. For example, the demand for cinema seats may decline because the demand for television sets goes up. Also the introduction of a new product or changes in the design of an old one may well affect the quantity demanded of another product. For example, the introduction of lightweight motor-cycles may create a demand for certain types of protective clothing for women. The change from the open 'touring' chassis to the closed saloon type motor-car caused a decrease in the demand for some types of men's protective clothing. The introduction of television caused changes in the demand for household furniture and food.

Changes of fashion, or what is sometimes called the 'spirit of the age' is subtly reproduced throughout the markets of a community. An age, in which the most highly regarded shape is slim and streamlined, besides producing slim aircraft, motor cars and trains for cheaper running will also produce slim clothing, refrigerators and radios at least partly for aesthetic reasons. A brown generation, or a pastel one, a highly stylised one, or a functional one, or an age of impressionism—all these represent changes of taste, fashion, fad, call it what you will, that affect the design of products offered for sale in a host of markets.

There are 'taste-changers' always in our midst. The business man who can bring about a significant change in taste in the direction of a product he is organised to produce is on the road to fame and fortune. All the time there are businesses presenting new products which they hope will oust the old from the market-place.

Some firms regard this process of changes in taste as inevitable —something that cannot be resisted and, therefore, to be carefully accommodated within organisation. So they do not wait for a rival taste-changer to kill their product with a new fashion. They create a new fad themselves, usually at the peak of the success of their current product, with the deliberate intent of ousting their own 'old-fashioned' product with their new up-to-date' product. Detergent manufacturers do this. Other undertakings have to do it, but more reluctantly. Airlines may have to introduce new aircraft that will ruin the demand for their older ones, just because their competitors are doing so. Publishers sometimes produce books that affect the sales of their existing stock just because if they did not someone else would.

There are two main ways in which disaster can overtake a business that is not prepared for change. Firstly, it can suddenly find that its organisation is no longer geared to produce what can be sold. It is no longer a fit instrument for the managerial purpose. It may have to be restaffed, retooled, re-equipped, or restocked with raw materials. This may take a long time and call for fresh capital. And a business caught on the wrong foot is not in the best position to ask for capital.

Secondly, it can find itself with stocks of its own product that have become valueless overnight. This sudden loss of value causes a sort of business anaemia, because as we have seen a business organisation is to a great extent self-financing. A constant supply of revenue is needed to maintain the elements of organisation. Unless there is a reserve to cushion such a blow, or the organisation can change quickly to earn revenue in a different way, it will begin to disintegrate. The business will begin to skimp on wages, replacement of equipment and so on, and things may go quickly from bad to worse.

I hope I have stressed sufficiently the imperative need for business organisation to be fully prepared for change. Every organisation should have a part of it entrusted with the special responsibility of sensing the need for change. If the organisation is big enough there is a strong case for having a special Development Manager whose job it is to remain watchful: to do this he may well have to remain aloof from the day-to-day pressures of the business. Someone who has to watch the way things are going—the direction of movement—needs to be patient, needs to be convinced of the value of just waiting, yet remain alert for the moment when it becomes clear that the time for action has arrived.

The same manager should be charged with the duty of successfully putting across to his colleagues his views on the prospects of change. It is no good if the organisational antenna is sufficiently sensitive to absorb all the signs of change, but is not capable of convincing others of the true significance of the signs. While organisation is carrying out its primary task of meeting the day-to-day needs of the customers of the business, someone must be constantly preparing it for change to meet the demands of the future. The development manager has to keep his organisation poised on the edge of change every day of its existence.

The development manager must have close relations with people inside the organisation who can supply him with information they have gleaned from their own external relations, and he must have his own external relations to promote the same end. The marketing manager is obviously one of his most important sources of information within the organisation. Outside the organisation he may have to keep in touch with a number of research institutions, technical press, and other specialist indicators of market trends.

From the information he collects, the development manager must deduce what is likely to follow and at the right time produce guides for a new design, and foster the organisational adjustments that will be needed to work to the new design.

One of the great difficulties of combining development with other functions, say production or marketing, is that the latter require a concentration of every sinew on making the organisation efficient as it is, whereas the former requires a spirit devoted to destroying what is. This conflict of attitudes is difficult for most men to accommodate, and points to the need for two sorts of men, one the doer and the other the innovator.

What I have said above is equally true when it comes to considering the changes that must be made in processes, equipment and raw materials, in order to be able to produce more cheaply. In a market where producers can compete by lowering prices the business that finds a cheaper way of making its product can capture the market. Even a temporary capture of the market, for the reasons we have already examined, can permanently cripple competitors. A single simple discovery can make the current production processes, skills, equipment and raw materials of all other businesses immediately obsolescent. So every business is compelled to engage in the restless search for improved methods, so that even if they do not all alight upon the same economy at the same time they may each discover something that will enable them to keep in business, even though it may be with reduced profits. This is so where there is real competition, but of course where there is no real competition a business can get away with out-of-date organisation.

If the case for having a special development manager begins with the need for every business organisation to pay particular attention to preparing for change, it ends with the problems of controlling research and development. It is quite usual to use these two words side by side when talking about what I have up to now called development, to indicate the study that precedes discovery and the task of application that follows it. It is helpful to my argument at this stage to emphasise the two parts of the job because what I have to say now is more generally true of research than it is of development.

People who take up careers in industrial research are in some ways unusual. They are different from most of us in the training they have received, and in the techniques they use in their daily work. The dilemma is this. A business organisation must keep its members on a fairly tight rein, otherwise organisation falls to pieces. Yet the nature of research and development is such that it requires a loose rein, if the most is to be made of the training and techniques of those engaged in it.

Research and development can very easily wander off beam. The curiosity and imagination of workers in it are a constant threat to the organisational intention of research. Research programmes easily begin to clog up production. This is partly because it is not easy to distinguish research from that which is not research, and research workers tend to get mixed up in the working machinery of business.

One of the devices for reconciling the claims of research and development staff for freedom, and the claims of management for organisational discipline is as follows. An expenditure budget is prepared to cover a particular period of activity. This has to fall into line with the business accounting period, but in its provisions allows for the fact that some research programmes cannot help but stretch over many accounting periods. Most of the money asked for in the budget is for fairly well-defined projects: the proposals for expenditure are sufficiently detailed for someone who is not a research man to be able to assess the validity of the estimates. But a margin of, say, a quarter of the total proposed expenditure is for unspecified work. This means that three-quarters of the research programme needs the prior approval of management, but one quarter of the programme is left to the discretion of the development manager, within a certain money limit. The part that needs prior approval is set out in such a way that it can be understood by general management, and in enough detail to enable management to exercise budget control throughout a programme. Time schedules may even be built into this part of the budget and status reports may be required from the research and development department at the end of each time period in the schedule, or at the end of each natural stage of the project.

The marginal part of the budget gives, it is hoped, enough freedom to allow the imaginative research worker to exercise his inventive talents, and at the same time to limit the freedom to what organisation will bear.

In my experience research people tend to behave oddly. Perhaps it is because they do not value the same things in life as we ordinary mortals. Their habits must be put up with, rather than encouraged in business. This is not too difficult if oddities can be confined to the real back-room boys. But it so often happens that the researchers must be supported by a greater number of clerks, secretaries, store-keepers and so on. It is absolutely essential that the normal organisational standards are applied to these supporting troops. Sharp contrasts in behaviour there may be. It is prudent to make the boundaries between the one sort of behaviour and the other as short as possible.

Part III

THE INDIVIDUAL MANAGER

'Neither his mother nor his school teacher had ever prepared him for so stern an ordeal—the fate of many another. Six months under a keen Captain, that's what he wanted. . . .'

HAMILTON

(*The Soul and Body of an Army*)

INTRODUCTION

This part of our study deals with what goes on inside the individual manager. As I said in the preface, organisation is essentially a task of getting relationships right. These relationships in business fall into three groups. Firstly, there are the relationships between those inside the business organisation and those outside it. Secondly, there are the relationships between various parts of the business, between man and man, and among men, equipment, and raw materials. And, thirdly, there are the relationships of the different characteristics of the individual manager: characteristics that are affected this way and that by the numerous and conflicting influences at work on them.

If a manager is a human wreck he will inevitably collide with other people in his organisation. These collisions will do further damage to himself and will do harm to other people. In the end the whole organisation can become a crazy pattern of damaged vessels set on collision courses. This may sound somewhat over-dramatised, but it is in fact a fundamental truth recognised by communities throughout history in the act of expelling the trouble-maker from their midst.

A man becomes a wreck because his various characteristics are no longer in tune with each other. His nature has become discordant. All his energies must be devoted to settling the trouble within himself, and he becomes less and less concerned with anything outside of himself. In sheer blindness of self-absorption he is incapable of steering himself through the crowded problems of daily business life.

The first chapter in this section examines the demands made upon a person by the task of managing. At the same time it shows up the strain that these various demands place upon the integrity of the individual. In a sense it indicates the constant tuning-up process necessary to keep individual characteristics in harmony.

The second chapter in this section deals with the source of supply of managers. It looks at the problem of finding men with the right endowments, and the right dispositions, and with the right skill and knowledge. And having found the right men, how can the training and education of a business environment develop these characteristics and keep them integrated?

The final chapter deals with the effect on the integrity of a manager of the rewards for his service to his business.

CHAPTER XIX

THE PERSON AND THE TASK

Much of what has already been said in Chapter X is a useful basis for the study of a manager's special position in organisation. The classification of human characteristics into endowments, disposition, skill and knowledge is as helpful in analysing the problems of the individual manager as it is of operatives.

Let us first remind ourselves of the salient features of a manager's task. He has to maintain certain external relations: with customers, with the State, with shareholders, suppliers and the public. He has to maintain a particular sort of relationship within the business that is peculiar to what we call organisation. He has to have a formalised relationship with unionised labour within his own business. He will also probably be involved in the distinctive relationship between one special manager and another. Finally, he is intimately concerned with the relationship between one characteristic and another, within himself.

When these relationships within a man are right we say he has integrity. This word comes from a Latin root which means entire or whole. Integrity is a condition in which the human being has no part wanting or impaired. This word was probably first used as long ago as 1450. But three centuries earlier this condition was recognised in the use of a word from which was derived the word 'wholesome'. Some surroundings and ways of living and working help a man keep his integrity; others make it more difficult for him. Unfortunately business, all too often, is one of the latter. The pressures that are brought to bear by the external and internal relations dealt with in the two previous sections will disintegrate the individual unless he is clever enough and strong enough, and rightly disposed to keep them in check.

Let us look first at what is required of the individual manager if he is to be successful in his external relations. His range of understanding and sympathy must be extraordinarily broad. Scholars in their professional lives deal mainly with scholars. Soldiers in their professional lives deal mainly with soldiers. But business men often have to deal with people from widely differing walks of life. A customer is a customer, whether he be cultured or not, intelligent or stupid, dishonest or not. Not only must the manager be able to read the minds of people without the same upbringing, training and interests as himself, but he must in turn be able to make himself understood by the customer, general public and so on.

It is very difficult to summarise in a few words the qualities that make for broad understanding and sympathy. But we can get fairly near by saying that the business manager must have a disposition that does not shrink from worldliness and that will enable him to temporise. His intellect must not exclude common sense, nor must noble thought rob him of the ability to be down-to-earth. He must be willing to deal with people, even to suffer fools gladly, and he must cause other people to be willing to deal with him, even if they are fools. At the same time the intelligence that is required for a complete mastery of the facts relevant to a business situation will in all probability have attracted him away from the everyday and commonplace. A fine intellect and a disposition to dabble in the ugliness and dirt that is business are uneasy bed-fellows. The strain is, I think, evidenced by the number of business men who occasionally yearn to quit the rough and tumble of business for quieter academic pursuits.

To maintain successfully the relations peculiar to organisation calls for another set of characteristics. If his whole organisation is not going to wobble, a manager must be capable of firm intention. Broadly speaking, there are two characteristic conditions that cause men to dither. One is the inability to make up one's mind in the first place, and the other is an inability to stick to a line of conduct even after one is convinced that it is right.

If a more intelligent man makes decisions they are likely to be better decisions than those that would have been made by a less intelligent man. It is also true that a more intelligent man would be able to sort out the relevant facts in a situation more quickly than would a less intelligent man, and as a result reach a decision more quickly. But it does not follow that because a more intelligent man is able to make better decisions when he makes them, and is capable of making good decisions more quickly, that he will in fact choose to make them readily.

There are some people who habitually take a long time to make up their minds about what to do because they are scrupulous by disposition. They tend for business to be over-nice or meticulous in matters of right and wrong. They will not do anything until they are quite convinced that they are proposing to do the right thing. Sometimes this is because they are afraid of the consequences of making a mistake, and will not take the risk. Or it may be that they are not disposed to compromise by embarking on a line of conduct that may be second best. Then again there are people who, even when they have begun a course of action with their intellect fully convinced that it is right, are easily shaken from it by emotional forces or sheer lack of guts in the face of opposition.

A manager must be capable of firm intention. This means he must be able to make up his mind to do something, even though he is not fully convinced that what he proposes to do is the best thing that could be done if all the facts were known. Very often something must be done before he has collected enough facts to convince himself. He must be prepared to turn out to be wrong some of the time. And once committed to a course of action, with his organisation geared up and set on it, he may well have to stick to it, even when fresh facts turn up to prove he should have done something else.

A manager must be able to plan to fulfil his intention. This means being able to mentally picture, step by step, and stage by stage, from beginning to end, the process for which he is responsible. Then he must be able to turn his mental picture into a map that other people can consult and understand. The maps may in parts be descriptive passages, in part standing orders and instructions. This calls for a mind that is capable of taking a whole task, and breaking it down into its component smaller ones, while preserving all the natural sequences by putting first things first. Not everyone is endowed with this incisive mental ability, nor has developed the methodical disposition that the detailed work calls for. It also calls for a mind that having indulged in these exceptional mental exercises is capable of putting its thoughts back into the vernacular.

Another characteristic required by the organisational relationships of a manager is the ability to exercise authority over human conduct to ensure the fulfilment of his plans. Recalling what was said in an earlier chapter, the meaning of authority is not restricted to the dishing out of orders. It has a wider meaning attached to authorship. A man of authority must be able to spark off the sort of conduct he wants. In order to initiate conduct in other people it may sometimes be necessary to inspire them, sometimes to suggest, sometimes to threaten, sometimes to punish. I am not forgetting that people will sometimes do the right thing if they are simply left alone, but it is impossible to rely on this in organisation. A manager must exercise authority.

Whether or not a person can exercise authority is, I think, largely the result of educational influences on disposition. It has something to do with endowments, but these only furnish the raw material for authority. Obviously, someone very dull and stupid is not likely to influence other people widely. But it is also true that a highly intelligent person may have no authority over others.

An inability to exercise authority springs from environmental circumstances that foster in an individual the belief that it is an exceptional exercise, improper most of the time, and bringing consequences that are to be feared. Children in many lower middle-class families have been brought up in a very tolerant family atmosphere and in state schools where authority is deliberately kept as unobtrusive as possible. Consequently they are hardly aware of the existence of authority, let alone its organic necessity. One of the great advantages of the English public school system is that, with its ingrained caste systems and layer upon layer of authorities that burden the lives of the new boys, it accustoms boys to the idea of authority and gives them practice in its exercise as they move up the school.

Some people have deep-seated political or doctrinal beliefs that the exercise of authority over others is improper. Some forms of democratic ideals and some forms of non conformist consciences cause people to shun authority. Some people have an ineradicable belief founded in a genuine humility that they are not worthy to influence other people. Very fine scholars have sought to avoid appearing to teach because they felt they had nothing to teach. Finally, there are those people who have bitter memories of harsh domineering parents and who do not wish other people to suffer what they suffered, or at least do not wish to be the object of a similar hate to that engendered within themselves by authority.

Whatever the cause of this particular incompetence, and however much we may sympathise with its origin, it is a serious shortcoming for a manager.

I have left until last in this list of characteristics required by the manager to maintain relations in organisation something that is usually referred to as 'organising' ability. This is an apt description of the characteristic, but it is not particularly helpful. Organising ability is partly to do with dividing up the task as we said above, but additionally it is to do with the way the elements of organisation are grouped. There is often a self-evident logic to compel an intelligent person to tackle a task in a certain order. There is not so often a clear 'best' way among the possible alternative groupings of men, equipment and materials.

Highly developed organising ability of this sort—that is combining the abilities to break down tasks and optimise the grouping of the elements of organisation—is rare. Fortunately it is not needed by every manager. Most of them can get by with the traditional groupings, but every so often a business needs the brilliant organiser, the man with a flair for the nicety of judgement that produces exactly the right organisation pattern at the critical moment.

Just as not all managers have occasion to exercise a very high degree of organising talent, not all managers need to have the skill and strength to resist the importunate demands of organised labour. But if a manager is to have anything to do with this sort of negotiation he does require exceptional characteristics. The best negotiators, in my experience, have been those whose imperturbable dispositions betray none of their reactions and keep the other side guessing what they are thinking. The courtly dance of offer and counter offer on the negotiating table is in many ways akin to the parleys that take place in international diplomacy. Talleyrand's advice to young diplomats— *pas trop de zèle*—should be carefully heeded by young managers concerned with industrial relations.

Before I attempt to summarise what I have said so far, I want to re-emphasise the danger of the division of characteristics. It is useful to give us some sort of mental grip on the subject of human characteristics, and what is needed by a manager. The danger is in thinking that because they have been divided in this way that they can be considered as exclusive members of their class. They cannot. They are interrelated. The exceptional endowment accompanied by a disposition to waste it will be less fruitful than a mediocre endowment accompanied by a disposition to use it fully. Skill and knowledge are related to mental and physical endowments and the dispositions that accompany them. Bearing this in mind, let us look at a summary of the endowments I believe to be necessary for a manager:

Adequate general intelligence
Common sense
Courage
Analytical ability
Ability to put difficult ideas into simple language
and exceptionally: A flair for 'organising'.

Something more must be said about two of these items: general intelligence and courage.

A person who has more general intelligence than another person has the following advantages. He can understand more easily. He catches the meaning or import (the consequence or importance) of something more easily. That is to say, its meaning or importance for things around it. The more intelligent person is more often accurate in his determination of the reasons why something is as it is. The more intelligent person is more likely to be able to to deduce what will happen next.

The sort of questions I would put to someone to test his intelligence in its application to a field of skill and knowledge in which he had adequate time to prepare would begin like this:

'Distinguish between . . . .'
'What steps can we take . . . ?'
'What are the main causes . . . ?'
'What is meant by . . . ?'
'Under what conditions may . . . ?'
'Compare the advantages and disadvantages of . . . .'
'Explain how . . . .'

'Give your opinion on . . . .'
'What would be the effect of . . . ?'
'What is the importance of . . . ?'
'Why is . . . ?'

For a long time questions beginning like this have been asked by school and university examiners to test intelligence. I believe that it is still the best way of doing the job. The disadvantage of the method is that it requires someone clever enough to be able to judge the answers.

Why list courage as an endowment? Is not courage a matter for will-power, and this would be classified as a disposition? I think not. Some people are saddled with irrational fears that are part of their psychological outfit. By disposition they may make the most of what little courage they have, and even accomplish 'brave' deeds. But being defective in this characteristic is a great handicap to a manager.

When we come to summarise the dispositions required by a manager we must begin with the overriding disposition to use the endowments that have been given. Then his dispositions should make him:

down to earth
willing to deal with people
not extremely scrupulous
willing to risk the consequence of mistakes
reasonably proof against emotions affecting judgements
methodical
willing to exercise authority
and exceptionally: imperturbable.

We can generalise as far as this on the characteristics required by a manager. Broadly speaking, the endowments and dispositions he requires are much the same whether he be a general manager or a special manager, a purchasing manager, or sales manager. We cannot, however, generalise so much beyond these two classes because skill and knowledge required does vary with the sort of management.

Thus a general manager requires to develop the skill of a judge, and a special manager the skill of an advocate. A development manager controlling a hundred scientists needs to exercise different skills from those of the manager controlling a thousand operatives. A sales manager must have different knowledge from the knowledge required by a finance manager, and so on.

If I am right, and it is valid to pick out certain human characteristics and say that these are required by a manager, to maintain the external and internal relations I have described, does it follow that there are certain threats to his integrity, inherent in the situation? The mere possession of the characteristics I have mentioned would not by itself spell ruin for someone's integrity. All I have said is that these characteristics have to appear in a manager's make-up. These few are the ones he needs to use as a manager. There are many others he needs to use as a father, or clubman, or churchman, and so on. All the characteristics that are needed for all the occasions together make him well integrated—nothing is missing. Something would be missing if only those characteristics required for successful management were possessed by the man. In that case he would not be well integrated.

There is a danger of any man becoming unbalanced, or disintegrating, if he is immoderate in the extent to which he allows himself to be absorbed by his 'occupation'. We all of us need to redress the balance of undue concentration upon the use and development of a small number of characteristics to our chosen career. So we must have adequate leisure and change of role. It is very dangerous to be too devoted to one's job. We must have other interests that make demands on other characteristics. Otherwise it is like a weight-lifter who, by concentrating on the use of a particular set of muscles, develops his physique disproportionately.

The disproportionate exercise of authority could, if there were no checks and balances, produce a petty tyrant. The disproportionate regard for intellect can produce arrogance, and so on. In this sense then the exercise of the select managerial characteristics can endanger the individual's integrity, but the common sense that is necessary for successful managers should steer a man through these shoals.

Assuming that there is no more than usual inherent danger in the way a manager must be personally equipped, is that the end of the matter? No, there is something else to consider. We have said enough in previous chapters to show that business organisation is subject to conflicting pressures, both from without and from within. The customers want one thing, the shareholders another, the general public another, and the State something else. These external relations are carried into the organisation and are strongly reflected in the nature of internal relations.

In the preface I used an orchestra as an analogy to illustrate the good relations that were necessary for complete harmony. What I did not say at that stage was about the conflict that may well be raging around the conductor. A bank manager may be pressing for better box-office receipts. Musicologists may be raging at his interpretations. The members of the orchestra may be pressing for wage increases. The accountants may be worried by the current policy for depreciating the instruments in the accounts of the orchestra. The medical profession has begun to issue warnings about the danger to health in blowing down trumpets. To yield fully to any single one of these claims might be disastrous to his other relations.

And so it is with the manager in business.

CHAPTER XX

THE MAKING OF MANAGERS

———

By the time a business comes to consider someone for employment much has gone into his making. Certain foundations, that we have called endowments, were at birth. But work on the foundations was not complete at that stage: all through the periods in the cradle, the nursery, and at school, the foundations were being strengthened, developed and extended. Some, but not all, human endowments may be fully developed by the age at which people leave school. Thus a young person may have grown to his full height, and very probably his general intelligence is as high as it will ever be, but he is still emotionally immature.

Besides these foundations at birth, in the early years other human characteristics are moulded in such a way that the overall pattern of 'character' is shaped one way or another. Some people believe that these early years, say from birth to seven years of age, are so important that if the child is properly taught during them he is proof against damaging influences in later years. It is during the early years that dispositions are moulded.

Now just how significant is this period of tutelage in the making of a manager? We will leave out of our discussion the person who unfortunately was poorly endowed at birth, and consequently had no sure foundations on which to build. We will confine our thinking to the person who was well enough endowed at birth, in the sense that, had the most been made of those endowments, within reason, he would have been capable of one day becoming a manager. Then to put the problem in perspective we must remember that there may be something like a ten-year gap between the time he enters business and when he puts his foot on the first rung of a management ladder.

G

This figure of ten years is arbitrary, but I think it not an unreasonable one for our present purpose.

The first question we might ask is how much that should have been, but was not, done during the first sixteen to twenty years, can be done within business organisation during the next ten? If, for example, someone has not been gradually introduced to the exercise of authority, or has not been made sociable while at school, can the deficiency be made up in business? Secondly, how much that was and should not have been done can be undone in the next ten years? For example, if someone has not only not been encouraged to be methodical, but has had years of bad example making them unmethodical, can business correct this? If the first eighteen years are moulding years, what chance has business of re-shaping a character in ten?

Secondly, if the answer is that business can do quite a lot to reshape the characters of most people, why should it run any of risks involved in not succeeding? Reshaping people's characters is not the job of business. It is an uneconomic activity. It is a cost that could have been avoided if one has chosen a person already well shaped for a successful business career.

This sounds fine. We can agree that it is sound business to choose those people who are already well made from the point of view of business; but however prudent we are and however much time we spend on choosing people we can never be sure that we have got what we thought we had. Assessing human characteristics can never be an exact science. We are bound to make mistakes. Business organisation must be framed on the premise that some mistakes in choosing men for jobs will be made.

The most reasonable attitude business can take is to regard its primary task as that of choosing those it thinks are already *most suited* for a successful career in business. It will usually take the added precaution of 'providing for wastage'. This term 'wastage' includes those who leave the firm for any reason, such as going to another firm, illness, death and so on. In this context it means anticipating the fact that some people will not make the grade in spite of the fact that it was thought that they would. If a business is too cautious and over-provides for this likelihood, then it may end with many more suitable people than it has jobs for. This is wasteful from the point of view of the community and damaging to the interests of some individuals.

There is not a surplus of people suitable to become managers, and we should regard it as anti-social to attempt to grab as many as we can find regardless of our needs. I believe that this is what is happening today in many large organisations. Particularly repellent are the large-scale hunting expeditions organised each year for the trapping of university graduates.

Partly because a number of businesses can attract most of the best, and partly because there are not enough well-developed applicants to go round anyway, many businesses are forced to take people whose development leaves much to be desired. Let me remind you that I am talking about people who were well enough endowed, but whose endowments were not made the best of *from the point of view of business*. I stress this point now because I do not want to suggest that someone not well developed for a business career is, *per se*, not well developed. What I mean is that a person who is well developed for an academic research career, or a teaching career, or an army career, may not be well developed for a business career. The fact that a person is in good shape for teaching or soldiering may well mean that he has developed some characteristics that are undesirable in business and, of course, vice versa.

Let us summarise what we have said so far. Making managers means developing something already in a person at birth. A lot of developing goes on between the time a person is born and the time he enters business. Although there is usually a gap of some years between the time a person enters business and the time he begins to assume managerial responsibilities, a prudent business will primarily aim to choose people who, from their point of view, have been well developed. Because of natural and artificial shortages this primary aim will not be achieved in many businesses. These must be prepared to remedy deficiencies in the individual development that took place before coming into business.

This is a sensible attitude for another reason. For some young people school can never be a good environment for their development. Those who mature more quickly than usual may find their last years at school unendurable because school organisation is based on the assumption that they are immature. This situation can easily affect a pupil's disposition to work so that he does not develop well in mental skill and knowledge. But the adult world of business, if used properly, can often quickly make up lost ground in cases like this. Used badly it can, of course, reinforce the tendencies developed at school.

School sometimes does not make the best of people. Business can sometimes succeed where school has failed.

Given that it is prudent for business to select the best developed people available, we must next ask whether there are any guiding lights? Are we more likely to find the young people with the best development (from the point of view of business) in any particular sort of school, coming from any particular sort of home, and so on?

It is very tempting to jump to conclusions merely in order to simplify the search. Some schools concentrate on developing their pupils' intellects. Others concentrate on characteristics like courage, willingness to exercise authority, willingness to take risks and so on. Probably no one school will ever fill the bill. General Certificate of Education results may be fair guides to general intelligence, but they do not tell us whether or not the possessor is disposed to like his fellow men, or even whether he is endowed with a due measure of common sense. Going to a certain school and passing certain examinations may help us to establish some facts in favour of a particular applicant. The danger lies in thinking that because we cannot establish the same facts *in the same way* with another person they are not true of him.

As a matter of policy it is wise to avoid the temptation to take short cuts by prejudging the product of certain types of school and family background. I would advise that all the available evidence be examined just as thoroughly no matter what school or family a person comes from.

School reports going back over a number of years are often a useful guide to development. In particular they often give clues to a young person's disposition. This information read against examination results may in turn give a valuable lead on his endowments. I am surprised how little business men use these school reports. Complete trust cannot be placed in any single report, but a number of them supporting each other may be taken as reliable evidence.

So far we have talked of the problem of choosing someone, whom we hope will one day be fit to be made a manager, whose only development has been outside of business, in the home and at school. When we come to consider a person who has already spent some years in business we face a situation with some important differences. In the first place the testing ground is apparently a truer one. After all, has not the man we are now looking at been able to show his paces in an environment that is strictly relevant to his application? Can we not see how he has developed in the right environment? Not necessarily. It still may not be on the managerial side of business. Sometimes the ranks of business are one of the poorest environments for the development of managerial characteristics. Sometimes, for example, a young person leaves school having exercised very considerable authority as a prefect for over a year or two. He then goes into business and has no command for years so that his disposition for it is weakened. He may be required to do routine work that weakens his intellectual ability and after some years in business he is less well developed than at the time he had finished schooling.

Secondly, although business should be able to provide a truer environment for development than say school, it is often much more difficult to find out what has happened to a person in business than it is to find out what happened to him at school. We may well decide that the evidence offered by the educational system on the development of an individual by its reports, examination results, awards of scholarships, prizes and offices is inconclusive. But we would have to admit that compared with the educational system, business is usually very haphazard in its approach to the problem. Some firms have developed good reporting procedures but they are few. Even the best firms will not trouble to furnish carefully prepared evidence to accompany the application from one of their employees for a post in another business. Very few business men, when they come to consider one of their own employees for promotion to a managerial post, can trust the evidence they have available. For example, in some of the most 'enlightened' undertakings it is impossible to find any evidence that is adverse to any employee, because a tradition has grown up that adverse reports are never given.

It is not altogether surprising that the educational system should usually be so much better than business in its assessment procedures. After all, the educational system is a vast piece of machinery geared to do this very thing. It is small wonder that its comparative expertise often dominates the story of a man's career. I have often witnessed a selection board devoting most of its time to discussing the education records of men who have been in business for over twenty years!

So this is the paradoxical situation we face. Because school is not like business, we must be guarded in our use of the evidence of development at school. But often service in the lower ranks of business is even less like business management than membership of the Sixth form at school is. Moreover, the evidence available on a person's development in business, in all but a few firms, falls far short of the standards of educational assessment. So we end up with a strong case for believing that we are less likely to make errors in judgement in choosing people for management on their school record than on their business record.

This is obviously an unacceptable position. Business must do something about it. The years between leaving school and the first managerial appointment are full of danger. Many of the advances made during school can be lost in the first five to ten years in business. Endowments should not be neglected. If they are not used they do not stand still at whatever particular stage of development they have reached. Like muscles that are not used they wither.

On the other hand business cannot afford to run great risks in order to secure the development of its young employees. This would defeat its purpose. Young people who are inexperienced generally cannot be entrusted with the sort of task that would do much for their development. Because of this they must be relegated for most of the time to less important, probably monotonous, routine tasks. I am not saying that business should take no risks in the interest of management development, but whatever risks are taken must be carefully calculated and kept well within bounds. It is the old story; you cannot allow the young apprentice to get in the hair of people busy on production. But the solution is not to leave the apprentice sitting day after day just watching.

The only solution possible if individual development is prevented by the works is to see that the development occurs elsewhere, away from the works. We have to create artificial 'business' problems on which to exercise intelligence. So we continue the educational processes of the school room to tide young people over the dreary beginnings in business. We must provide somewhere an invigorating climate so that one day when his experience in business is adequate a young person can begin to apply his endowments to the problems of business. The thinking techniques we acquire at school cannot be applied in business until we have come to understand business thoroughly. It would be like the man who had learnt to use a chisel on plain deal and believed that this made him ready to tackle oak and teak.

This is why continuing to study for examinations is in a sense a valuable outlet. The subject-matter of these academic studies may not seem to be particularly relevant to business and business management, but the processes involved are very relevant to the development of the individual.

I must now say some more about dispositions. I do not think these are likely to suffer so much in the early years in business as endowments are. The example of seniors plays a very important part in the development of the disposition of a young person. So that the monotony and routine nature of his own task does not prevent the development of characteristics that come by good infection from others, a disposition to be down-to-earth, to be willing to deal with people, to risk the consequences of mistakes and so on, may be fostered in the business 'nursery'.

The best sort of conditions might appear to be an odd mixture of the old-fashioned and the modern. We would find a code of manners reminiscent of the old-world courtesy of English business houses of the last century. There would be a certain formality in people's conduct and the observance of etiquette. There would be a noticeable insistence on obedience to instructions and on the maintenance of outward marks of respect. We would find it modern in the sense that new techniques of business were readily considered and adopted if proved sound.

Now we must look at the problem of developing in business the remaining two classes of human characteristics. We can safely assume that basically the skill and knowledge required for business management is developed by experience. But experience will remain inchoate unless it is illuminated by reflection and made orderly by being fitted into a mental scheme. It is necessary to provide some theory or system of ideas against which to see each bit of experience as it comes up.

The trouble with experience is not so much that it takes a long time to get, but that it is usually got in the wrong order. The mass of experience a man accumulates during a managerial career cannot be parcelled out to him in an ideal manner. If we were planning a 'programme' of experience it would be based on certain principles. It would lead him from small beginnings out to the undiscovered ends. He would move from easy situations progressively through more and more difficult ones. It would be well balanced in that he saw something of all aspects of managerial work as quickly as possible to give him an idea of the whole into which he will fit as part. But this is not how it happens in practice. Experience will come to him in a random fashion. He will be rather like the man who has to take a long journey on foot. He will face a lot of difficult country and a lot of easy country. He cannot rearrange the country so that he can tackle the really difficult bits when he has hardened himself and learnt a few tricks. He must take the features as they come, and his most helpful piece of equipment will be a map which will stop him getting lost, which will warn him about and help him to identify features much more quickly, and which will enable him to 'see' beyond the next hilltop. At the end of his journey he will not have trodden more than a tiny fraction of the area shown by his map, but with the sense that his map made of his experience, that experience will enable him to picture the whole territory from the map.

I believe that a person should be given his map early in his management career. It is as well that it is not immediately he becomes managerial because, unlike the walker, at first he can 'see' backwards only. He must have covered some territory before he can view it and identify it on a map. After a few months and within two years of his first managerial appointment he should be given a system of thought, or a framework and pegs on which to hang his subsequent experience.

Then the manager should go away and gain more experience. As he gains it bit by bit he can fit it into a pattern which will enable him to appreciate the significant aspects of each bit. He will be able to make the most of his experience.

After another two to three years' experience he should take time off again to re-examine the whole of his additional experience in the light of the system of thought that he was given at the beginning. The purpose of this re-examination should be to test the framework to see if it is strong enough to contain all his experience; to see if it places emphasis in the right places;

to see if it puts things in the right order; to see that it puts sign-posts where they were most needed.

At intervals after this second period of prolonged study, I think it is necessary to pause at intervals and spend time on specially difficult or changing aspects of the managerial task. It is possible at this stage to narrow the field of vision by specialisation. Early management studies need to be broadly based to support a variety of experience but later studies can afford to be taken in depth without loss to general under-standing.

To summarise then, management development in business should be taken in the following six stages:

1. Continuing discipline of academic studies during early years of 'routine' in business.
2. Short introductory experience in first managerial post.
3. Acquiring a framework of ideas.
4. Accumulating further experience.
5. Examining whole of accumulated experience in light of framework of ideas.
6. Taking a look at special aspects of a managerial task.

Stages two to five should take up to five years and stage six would be at intervals after five years' experience.

The making of managers is a slower process than we care to think. It will turn out to be even slower if we care not to think and plan development.

CHAPTER XXI

REWARDS FOR MANAGERS

If we are to avoid the deep divisions that often occur between management and men we shall have to do some serious thinking on the subject of rewards for managers. Whatever rewards are given to managers must be seen to be clearly justifiable. The 'we' and the 'they' cannot remain a distinction of privileged and under-privileged, rich and poor. It is obvious that the same human passions of greed, envy and hate unleashed by the follies of certain social and political organisations can find breeding ground in the circumstances of business organisation. It is not fashionable to talk of business and morality in the same breath, but business cannot be divorced from morality.

The answer some economists make to the problem of what should be the rewards of a manager will not satisfy the much broader thinking of our times. Their answer begins with the assumption that managers are scarce, that there are too few of them to satisfy all the needs. From this it follows that all businesses will be in competition with each other for what is available, and inevitably some businesses are going to have to do without. It is further assumed that such businesses make shift without proper management.

Because of the scarcity of managers a business can get a manager only by attracting him from some other business. Therefore, the rewards to management must always be above what those businesses making shift without proper management would be prepared to pay in order to secure managers. Furthermore, the highest bidder will obtain the best managers and others will get only what they pay for.

This system is justified on the grounds that the businesses that can afford to attract managers are the more successful ones, and the business that can afford to attract the best managers is the most successful. If we then assume that a business is successful in proportion to the extent to which it satisfies social needs in the shape of demands of the consumer, we can argue that by this system managers are automatically attracted to those businesses that are relatively better at satisfying social needs. By the same argument an individual manager may judge whether he is employing his talents to the best advantage by asking himself if he could earn more by working for another business. If he could earn more by working elsewhere then he should do so because it means that he is needed more elsewhere. Only by going to the highest bidder for his service can he be sure that he is servicing the greatest social need.

In this way managerial salaries are fixed not so much by the arbitrary decision of those in control of the business, but by the consumer of the product.

This argument has an element of truth in it, but it over-simplifies the situation and is misleading for a number of reasons. It begins with the basic mistake of thinking that a man is not a manager unless he is a good manager.

The 'scarcity' in the economist's argument is artificially intensified by using the term manager as a term of praise rather than as a matter of fact. A man is a manager because he is put into a situation in which he is given certain authority. Not all managers possess the well-developed characteristics of good managers. So while we may argue that *good* managers are scarce we cannot argue with equal force that *all* managers are scarce. In reality there is not a strictly limited number of managers available as assumed by the economists' argument. Businesses have available in the ranks of their workers, men whose characteristics can be developed sufficiently to make them suitable for management. Businesses can also draw their managers from many other walks of life, from the armed forces, the civil service, local government and the professions. The picture of businesses competing for a limited number of men already within a closed community is altogether too simple.

So while we may agree that the rewards of some managers of exceptional ability are determined by their selling their services to the highest bidder, it does not follow that the rewards of the great majority of managers are determined in this way. Employers are not restricted to bidding for a fixed supply; they may choose to bring in fresh supplies of managers from other sources.

However serious are the shortcomings of the economic argument as an explanation of how managers are rewarded, they are nothing to its failure to justify the process. Ordinary workpeople will never acknowledge the fairness of a situation in which a manager draws *personal* advantage from a situation that looks to them rather like an auctioning of human talents. They will demand from managers standards that are higher than their own. Even if they are prepared to indulge taking advantage of labour shortages they do not expect managers to sink to the same level.

And there is something to be said for their attitude. Why should a gifted man who has enjoyed the advantages of a good education behave as if his gifts were his own personal property? Why should he believe for a moment that his situation is to his credit and that the world owes him something for being what he is? Many organisations, civil and military, as well as professional bodies have long held the view that exceptional skill and education place a heavy obligation upon the individual to use his natural gifts and what he has acquired from the community primarily for the benefit of others and not himself. These organisations expect to attract men of first-class ability, but at the same time have developed codes to discourage the self-seeker. They constantly emphasise the idea of duty and curb the claims of privilege. They expect a high degree of selfless service from their members.

There seems to be no valid reason why business managers should not be expected to adopt the same attitude, and to have the same demands made upon them.

These ideals still have room for reasonable discussion of what should be the standards of reward of management. Working from the basic principle that a manager has the same right to expect to earn a living as any other man, we may still ask what standard of living? If it is different from that of workpeople, then why?

One of the main considerations in deciding what should be a manager's standard of living is the need to avoid wasting his abilities. It is the lot of the vast majority of mankind to have to pinch and scrape, which means that they are preoccupied with the struggle to get enough to eat, clothe and shelter themselves.

This preoccupation with mere subsistence is restrictive on imagination and creative thinking. It consumes time that could be spent on matters that contribute to the common good; it absorbs part of the limited energy of any man, and may even cause anxieties that encroach on all his activities.

If it is vital for a man to come to his work with a fresh, untroubled mind then it is folly to place the burdens of impoverishment upon him during the intervals he is at home. And a manager is a man who should come to work stripped for action, stripped of his own concerns, and ready to devote his energies to the problems of other people. The more devoted he is required to be the more he must be relieved of concern for his own welfare.

This then is a guide for establishing minimum reward. We have already considered some of the aspects that should influence the upper limits of a manager's rewards. Broadly speaking, we have said that if managers appear to take undue advantage of their situation by scrambling for material prosperity they will contribute to industrial unrest. We must add that beyond a certain point material rewards will corrupt and clutter a mind that should be largely freed of thoughts of personal gain.

APPENDIX

Some readers may find it useful to revise the ground covered in each chapter, by putting to themselves the questions contained in this appendix. Often the most useful part of a course of study is the questions that are asked, not the answers that are given.

Certainly not all the answers to all the questions are given in the text of this book. But in our present state of knowledge the question, 'What does a manager have to think about?', is answered more adequately by a host of other questions than by any book full of statements.

Questions

PREFACE

1 Give your opinion on the place of theory in the training of a manager.

2 What are the arguments for and against regarding 'management' as a *subject* of study?

3 What, if any, are the practices and skills that distinguish management from other human activities?

4 Give an outline of the relationships that must be considered in a study of management.

CHAPTER I

1 Illustrate from your own experience differences in the extent and nature of various managers' personal dealings with customers.

2 To what extent is it true that businesses selling services require different manager/customer relations from those selling goods?

3 What sort of manager/customer relations are likely to have adverse effect on business organisation?

4 Compare the advantages and disadvantages to a manager in his obtaining a customer's opinion on the conduct of a business.

Questions—CHAPTER I *continued*

5   Explain how a manager can set a good example in his relations with customers.

6   Comment on the legal relationship of manager and customer.

7   What are the likely effects of the monopolistic character of some businesses on their manager/customer relations?

8   Compare the advantages and disadvantages of appointing a special manager to deal with customer relations.

9   Give your opinion on Consumer Councils.

CHAPTER II

1   Give your opinion on the amount of influence that can be exercised by the individual manager on his relations with the State.

2   How did the *laissez-faire* policy of the nineteenth century affect business management of the time?

3   What were the main causes of the early State intervention in the affairs of business in the nineteenth century?

4   Discuss the significance of the 1875 Conspiracy and Protection of Property Act.

5   In what sense could the Trade Disputes Act of 1906 be regarded as a turning-point in industrial relations?

6   Compare the advantages and disadvantages of State mercantilist policy from the point of view of business management.

7   'A knowledgeable and skilful intermediary can greatly help a manager in his relations with the State.' Comment.

8   What are the main arguments in favour of present day State regulation of the conduct of business?

9   Discuss the role of government inspectors in business.

10   What would be the effect of extending the legal liability of managers for misconduct of business?

11   Comment on the special position of a manager in a Nationalised Industry from the point of view of his relations with the State.

CHAPTER III

1   Discuss the opportunities that managers of businesses of various sizes and types have to meet their shareholders.

2   What are the causes of shareholders:

    (*a*) remaining indifferent, and

    (*b*) taking an undue interest in the day-to-day conduct of the business in which their money is invested?

3   In what way does the concept of a perpetual group of shareholders influence managers to make decisions that damage the interests of the individual shareholder?

4   Discuss the role of management in balancing the interests of shareholders and the business organisation.

5   Explain how you identify the general public from the point of view of business.

6   What is the importance of the work of the public relations officer in business?

CHAPTER IV

1   Discuss the role of specialists in the external relations of business.

2   How far is it practicable to distinguish the offices of Chairman and Managing Director by making each primarily concerned with either internal or external relations of business?

3   What are the main organisational deficiencies that give rise to unfavourable impressions in the minds of people having dealings with a business?

4   What is likely to be the effect on external relations of bad morale among the employees of a business?

CHAPTER V

1   What is the importance of regarding the organisation of a business as separable from the business itself?

2   'It does not follow that more highly organised business is more orderly, harmonious and so on, or that less organisation must lead to muddle and discord.' Comment.

Questions—CHAPTER V *continued*

3 Why are business organisations sometimes regarded as ends in themselves?

4 Give an account of the elements of organisation.

5 Describe the processes of setting up a business organisation.

6 What are the main causes of failure in business organisation?

CHAPTER VI

1 'There are ways of doing business with organisation. There are ways of doing business without.' Comment.

2 What would you regard as the key areas in which a theory of organisation is required?

3 Explain the way costs operate to cause a business man to organise instead of contract. Is cost the only likely influence on his decision?

4 What are the theoretical limits to the size of organisation?

5 Are there any theoretical guides to the order in which organisation should occur?

6 What are the factors that determine the proportion of physical elements in organisation?

7 What is the effect of the proportion of physical elements upon the link elements of organisation?

8 Explain the circumstances in which the optimum size of organisation does not coincide with the optimum size of business.

9 An organisation tends to grow to a point where its rate of production will give the maximum profit to be obtained solely in organisation. Comment.

10 What is the importance of the concepts of average and marginal costs in the determination of the optimum size of an organisation?

11 Illustrate from your own experience the working of the rule of comparative advantage in determining the order in which activities are subordinated in organisation?

12 'The true costs of raw materials reflect the costs of preparing and finishing outside of organisation.' Comment.

13 How can we indicate the extent to which a business is organised?

CHAPTER VII

1   The sum of money spent on using operatives and equipment does not by itself show how much organisation there is. Comment.

2   The money spent on the use of the physical elements does not represent the full bill for organisation. Comment.

3   Organisation costs are not costs in the sense that they represent how much extra one has to pay for having organisation. Comment.

4   Analyse the costs of contracting.

5   Why does a business choose to spend money on other organisations?

6   What is the importance of the situations of falling constant and rising costs in determining whether to do business by organisation or by contracting?

7   Why do marginal costs vary?

8   What are the advantages of specialisation?

9   Illustrate from your own experience the benefits that flow from specialisation.

10   What are the main causes of rising costs?

CHAPTER VIII

1   Give an account of the relationship between superior and subordinate.

2   Compare and contrast the development in England of theories on the source of political power with the development of ideas on the source of authority within industry.

3   Has Lord Acon's dictum on the corrupting influence of power any application within industry?

4   Management authority should be based on the law of the land. Comment.

5   In what sense can authority be passed on?

6   Are there any techniques for assessing the distribution of authority in a business organisation?

7   Authority can be delegated, but responsibility cannot. Comment.

8   Is it possible to confine management authority and responsibility within economic bounds?

CHAPTER IX

1   Illustrate the various ways of grouping the physical elements of organisation.

2   What are the bases upon which organisational groupings may be made in business?

3   Illustrate the conditions that give rise to particular methods of grouping within business organisation.

4   Discuss the importance of the concept of association links and authority links in business organisation.

5   Compare the advantages and disadvantages of establishing several layers of authority in a business organisation.

6   What are the major kinds of tasks that are involved in the overall activity of running a business?

CHAPTER X

1   Give an account of the problems concerned with integrating the physical elements of organisation.

2   What are the problems associated with predicting the behaviour of a human being?

3   Outline a classification of human characteristics that you would regard as helpful in discussion of business needs.

4   Distinguish between endowments and disposition.

5   Distinguish between skill and knowledge.

6   What principles should govern the attitude of a business towards working conditions for its employees?

7   There is more likelihood of wasting human beings than of wasting equipment or raw materials. Comment.

8   What is the importance to a business organisation of its policy on issues like sick pay, holidays, career prospects, retirement age, pensions and so on?

9   What is the importance of establishing a system of feed-backs on the success or otherwise of managerial control over the human element in organisation?

10   What is your opinion of the place of rules and regulations in a business organisation?

CHAPTER XI

1   Analyse the economic standpoints of the parties to a wage settlement.

2   What is the importance of the concept of the employer's surplus?

3   What place has job evaluation among the general ideas that underlie wage settlements?

4   What is your opinion on the practicability of relating wages to the skill and effort put into a job?

5   Write a note on each of the following:
time-rates, piece-rates, incentive schemes, waiting time.

6   Compare the advantages and disadvantages of allowing wages to reflect the relative bargaining positions of employer and employee.

7   What are the main physical factors that are thought to influence productivity, contentment and health?

8   Explain the paradox of situations where workers respond to appeals for exceptional effort and succumb to complaining about trivial discomforts.

9   Give an account of the main differences in the distribution of power in trade unions.

CHAPTER XII

1   What are the bases for the distinction between general and special management?

2   At what levels in business organisation is general management usually found?

3   Give an account of the position of the general manager *vis-à-vis* superior and subordinate special managers.

4   What are the main causes of failure in the relationship between general and special managers?

5   Compare the advantages and disadvantages of recruiting general managers from the ranks of special managers.

6   Why is a connection between general and special manager often a very weak part of business organisation?

CHAPTER XIII

1   Give an account of the main business activities that fall within the special management field of finance.

2   What is the importance of decisions regarding the provision of capital for business?

3   What steps can a finance manager take to protect the capital invested in his business?

4   What is the importance to a business of the ease or otherwise with which investors may withdraw their funds?

5   What in your opinion is the part that should be played by a finance manager in determining the price that should be paid for money borrowed?

6   How do the elements of organisation depend upon decisions of finance management?

7   What sort of methods are used by finance managers to ensure that money fed into a business organisation is not wasted or used in an unauthorised manner?

8   What are the problems concerned with calculating and distributing the profits of a business?

9   Unrealistic book-values benefit no one but the speculator. Comment.

10   Distinguish between management and financial accounting.

11   What are the bases for organisational groups in finance divisions of business?

CHAPTER XIV

1   By the very nature of their specialisation, purchasing managers and production managers are committed to contracting and organisation respectively. Comment.

2   Under which conditions may the purchase of capital equipment be delegated to a special purchasing manager?

3   What are the problems associated with the purchase and stocking of spares?

4   What is the importance of the contractual relationship established by a purchasing manager between a business and its suppliers?

5   What are the basic approaches to the task of purchasing raw materials?

6   Suggest three alternative methods of organising a purchasing division of a business.

CHAPTER XV

1   What are the grounds for managerial specialisation in finance?

2   What are the grounds for managerial specialisation in purchasing?

3   Give an account of common fallacies concerning the nature of production in business.

4   Give your opinion on the most useful way in which to regard production.

5   Production is matching what is done with what is wanted and will be paid for. Comment.

6   What is meant by the statement that production is a residual activity?

7   What are the difficulties in defining the production aspects of business?

8   Explain how difficulties of measurement arise from difficulties in defining production.

9   Explain how managerial specialisation on production is justifiable on the grounds that production problems are those that are peculiar to a particular business.

CHAPTER XVI

1   Why is it that marketing may have a disproportionate effect on the prosperity of business?

2   Give an account of the problems concerned in the choice of a market-place.

3   What are the main causes of difficulties in deliveries to the market-place?

4   Distinguish between the situations in which a business sells:

      (*a*) at a market price, and

      (*b*) at a monopoly price.

5   What is the importance in marketing of the task of displaying wares?

6   What is the importance of paying careful attention to the way a business collects cash from its customers?

7   What are the main causes of complaint concerning deliveries from market to customer?

8   Discuss the position of the marketing manager in business organisation.

9   What is the effect of differences in processes of production on the approach of the marketing manager to his task?

CHAPTER XVII

1   What are the difficulties of having a personnel manager in a business organisation?

2   Compare and contrast the laws governing the behaviour of materials with those governing the behaviour of human beings.

3   What organisational difficulties spring from the nature of the laws governing human conduct?

4   Is it right to argue that the attention required by the human element in organisation is more than most business managers have time for, and therefore personnel management is a necessity?

5   What in your opinion are the activities that should be included in the responsibilities of a personnel manager?

6   What are the advantages and disadvantages of having a specialist to consider human limitations when planning organisational changes?

7   What in your opinion are the dangers of pressing the claims of humanity too far in business?

8   The sifting of grievances is one of the most important tasks of personnel management. Comment.

9   What is the effect of the division of business and consequent specialisation upon the career prospects of an individual?

10   The larger the organisation the more dangerous it is to rely upon the memory and opinion of any one man. Comment.

11   How much more important than money are the endowments, dispositions, skills and knowledge of a human being, and these are what a man or woman invests in a business that he or she goes to work for. Comment.

CHAPTER XVIII

1   What is meant by the development function of business?

2   What are the variable features in the demand for the products of business and which of these features would be the concern of a development manager?

3   Explain how changes in general purchasing power, and changes in economic preferences can affect the individual business. What can a development manager do to anticipate these changes?

4   What are the possible consequences of a business failing to prepare itself for change?

5   Give your opinion on the best way of describing the job of a development manager.

6   What are the problems associated with the managerial control of research and development staff and what special devices are employed to solve them?

CHAPTER XIX

1   Summarise all the relationships involved in the managerial task.

2   What is the meaning of integrity and has it any relevance to a discussion of managerial qualities?

3   What personal defects are likely to cause difficulties to a manager in his external relations?

4   What in your opinion are the characteristics required by a manager for the successful handling of his relationships within organisation?

Questions—CHAPTER XIX *continued*

5   Illustrate from your experience the endowments of successful managers.

6   What is meant by general intelligence? Discuss its importance as an endowment for managers.

7   Attempt a summary of the dispositions required by a manager.

8   A manager's skill and knowledge must be closely related to the peculiarities of his business and his own position within that business. Comment.

9   What are the dangers to a manager of his becoming preoccupied with the affairs of business?

10   Explain how it might be argued that one of the most important managerial tasks is to avoid yielding to any one of the many pressures exerted on management.

CHAPTER XX

1   What is the importance of the home and school environment for the early development of characteristics that suit a person for business management?

2   Give your opinion on the policy a business should pursue regarding the development it expects of its employees on recruitment.

3   The most reasonable attitude business can take is to regard its primary task as that of choosing those it thinks are already most suited for a successful career in business. Comment.

4   What steps can we take to ensure that the years between leaving school and obtaining a responsible position in business provide opportunities for the development of managerial characteristics?

5   What are the advantages and disadvantages of the school environment from the point of view of developing characteristics which suit people for business management?

6   Do any particular types of schools provide comparatively good environment for the development of characteristics that suit people for business management?

7   Compare the advantages and disadvantages of using examination results as evidence of development preparatory to business.

8 Give your opinion on the use that is made of school reports by selectors of candidates for business.

9 Compare the advantages and disadvantages of using the record of a number of years in business in choosing people who are expected to become managers.

10 What would be the effect on his development of a young person's spending his first few years in business on routine tasks?

11 Discuss the case for a young person's continuing academic studies during the first few years he spends in business.

12 Under what conditions may the right disposition for management be developed in business?

13 The trouble with experience is not so much that it takes a long time to get, but that it is usually got in the wrong order. Comment.

14 What steps can we take to make the most of experience in business management?

CHAPTER XXI

1 Are there any reasons for treating the subject of rewards for managers any differently from that of rewards for other classes of employees?

2 Compare the advantages and disadvantages of leaving the settlement of managerial rewards to the natural working of economic laws.

3 Is the belief that businesses are competing for a strictly limited supply of managers correct?

4 The interests of the business are best promoted by giving free rein to the self-interest of its managers. Comment.

5 Are there any guides for establishing minimum rewards of managers?